PRAISE FOR *MY GOODNESS: MY KIDS*

"An awesome read. Don't start this book on a day that you have plans. You will find yourself spellbound by Nesta's words and her skillful and successful parenting style."

—Marcia Essig, PhD

My Goodness: My Kids is an intimate portrait of an endangered species… a functional family. Nesta Aharoni serves up chapter after chapter of parental wisdom, each filled with practical techniques that can be put to use before you finish reading the book.

—Joshua Levitt, N.D.

"My goodness! It is really good. This book contains comprehensive, individually tailored, child rearing strategies that present a relatively simple and realistic method for producing honorable, educated, and happy adults."

—Bill Williams, PhD, author of *Trading Chaos*

"I can hear the author's gentle and directed voice in her flowing words of concern and logic. In a sea of volatility, this book offers an island of reprieve and reflection."

—Rabbi Ben Kamin

"The road to good parenting is filled with twists and turns and unpaved territory. Nesta Aharoni sheds light, direction, and good old homespun wisdom to help us find our way. A delightful, thought-provoking, and instructive read for what we all want in our lives—good kids."

—Bonita Pollen, M.A.

"Reading Nesta's book was a joyous opportunity. I especially appreciated the non-threatening diversions used in restaurants and other public places. But probably the clearest and most sensible advice in her parenting book is to choose the right spouse. Parents who are united make difficult child-rearing decisions a little bit easier."

—John A. Roach, Ed.D., District Superintendent CUSD

My Goodness:
My Kids

Cultivating Decency in a Dangerous World

My Goodness:
My Kids

Cultivating Decency in a Dangerous World

No Curfews, No Timeouts—No Violence, No Drugs

Nesta A. Aharoni

Grassroots Publishing Group, Inc.
Carlsbad, California
www.GrassrootsPublishingGroup.com

Grassroots Publishing Group, Inc.
300 Carlsbad Village Dr., Ste 108A #116
Carlsbad, CA 92008-2999
www.GrassrootsPublishingGroup.com
info@GrassrootsPublishingGroup.com

Unattributed quotes from *20,000 Quips & Quotes* by Evan Esar

First Edition 2008

Printed in the United States of America
Cover photo by Glenn Rivera
Cover & book design by CenterPointe Design

ISBN: 978-0-9794805-0-8

Library of Congress Control Number: 2007905601

DEDICATION

*I dedicate this book to my children Ilan, Eyal,
and Galia. I am in awe of you.*

*I also dedicate this book to my husband, Eitan.
Your decency has been the greatest
influence in my life.*

DISCLAIMER

The purpose of this book is to entertain and inspire parents who are seeking to raise good children in today's challenging world. It is sold with the understanding that Grassroots Publishing Group, Inc., (Publisher) and Nesta A. Aharoni (Author) are not engaged in rendering professional therapeutic advice. If expert assistance is required, the services of a competent professional should be sought.

It is not the purpose of this book to reprint information that is otherwise available to parents, but instead to complement, amplify, and supplement those texts with one family's stories of lessons learned. You are urged to read other available material on child rearing, learn as much about parenting as you can, and tailor the information gleaned to your personal needs.

Parenting results unfold slowly over time. Anyone who expects to parent effectively must invest a lot of thought and effort into it. This book is intended to encourage parents to expend energy forming their own unique, common-sense approaches to child rearing. Success, or lack of it, is based on many factors—some of which are out of a parent's control.

The author's intention is to encourage readers to use this book as a motivational tool to formulate their own parenting plans.

The purpose of this book is to entertain and motivate. Neither the Author nor the Publisher shall have liability or responsibility to any person or entity with respect to any loss or damage caused, or alleged to have been caused, directly or indirectly, by the use of information contained in this book for any purpose other than the entertainment of the reader.

The Author and Publisher waive liability or responsibility for the accuracy or completeness of information provided in the book. Further, the Author and Publisher waive liability to the reader or any other parties for any action taken based on reliance on information contained within the book or for any consequential, special, or similar damage.

ACKNOWLEDGMENTS

The publication of this book required team effort. I am honored to thank and acknowledge the players who helped create this book.

Jonathan Hulsh and Rabia Barkins, for their honesty, knowledge, and interest. By laying out the challenges on a restaurant napkin, you helped create a vision and motivated me to act. Samantha Marlowe, for your review and comments. Your friendship has enhanced my life. Glenn Rivera, for lending your creative talent to this endeavor. I delight in your photo images LeAnne Mellon, for being my muse. Your enthusiasm has carried me through many stages of life. Matthew and Joan Greenblatt of CenterPointe Design, for your artistic flair and your professional expertise. You have gone above and beyond in our relationship. You have become my partners in planning, production, and promotion. Phyllis Kahaney, Ph.D., and Terrin Irwin, for your editorial suggestions. Mirra Novak-Smith, for helping me to develop the confidence and mastery to bring this manuscript to its fruition. Jackie Valdez, for your foresight and optimism. You made me believe my book idea would become a reality.

Ilan, Ruth, Amir, and Noam Aharoni, for inspiring me to write this book. While living your daily lives, you display goodness, character, and all of the other qualities I hold dear. Eyal Aharoni, for your content contributions and constant support. You made me think—more than I wanted to sometimes. You naturally model integrity, steadfastness, and generosity. Galia Aharoni, for letting me know when something I wrote was "cheesy." Your insight and fresh ideas kept me going. Your commitment to justice and decency has been an inspiration. Eitan Aharoni, for helping me believe that my ideas were important, and for showering me constantly with love and encouragement. I treasure the trust you placed in me. Your example has been imprinted in our children's character, and for that I am deeply grateful.

CONTENTS

FOREWORD

I sit in front of my computer writing the Foreword to *My Goodness: My Kids* at a most curious time. My words coincide with the announcement that Britney Spears' 16-year-old sister, the star of the most popular TV show for 9- to 14-year-olds, is pregnant. And the book their mother has written, on parenting, has been put on hold. Perhaps that book, if it is ever published, will be full of wise and thoughtful information on child rearing. Perhaps.

What I know with certainty is that *this* book is full of wisdom and sage advice. It is replete with insights derived from trial and error. I say it is a "wise" book. I do not say that any or all of Nesta's parenting approaches are "correct" or "right." No one can. People have been opining and disagreeing about proper and effective parenting since the dawn of time.

I feel quite confident saying that this book is full of perceptive viewpoints about raising decent children. My confidence stems from the fact that I have inside information. I've watched Nesta

Aharoni's three children grow into adulthood over the last 20 years. They are extraordinary. On the surface, they are very unalike. However, at their core, they represent and reflect the goals that all parents share—to raise honorable, respectable, and productive citizens of the world.

I can see the three Aharoni children sitting together and engaging in a lively debate about whether their mom and dad's parenting approach is the reason they turned out as they have. The eldest, the most traditional of the three, soberly says, "Of course. The fact that each of us shares the same values of honesty and integrity cannot be mere coincidence." The middle child, the rational scientist, says, "A sample size of three is completely inadequate to draw any reliable conclusions about something as complex as child rearing. It would be impossible to control enough of the variables to even get close to a sensible conclusion." The youngest child, the aspiring lawyer, eagerly takes both sides of the argument and pushes them to their logical conclusions.

Some large questions can never be answered with complete conviction. But I have a hard time thinking that the results here are simply coincidence.

—The Honorable Stephen E. Hjelt, Administrative Law Judge

PREFACE

The world is saturated with highly educated professionals and specialists of every kind. And they contribute greatly to the maintenance and productivity of society. Yet there is something to be said for good, old-fashioned common sense—what I call *lay wisdom*. I have heard several people say that they would rather be guided by 100 random people whose names were pulled out of the local phone book than by 100 experts in a particular field. And I have to admit, I agree.

Lay wisdom is insight that is gained through living in, struggling with, and experiencing the world around you. It is not based on theory. It is grounded in real life. Lay wisdom is incorporated into our knowledge base after we grapple with situations, choices, and dilemmas. Is being late for work an excuse to cut another car off on a crowded freeway? Is coming home depleted after a rough day an excuse to treat other family members with disregard? Is saving for a home purchase an excuse not to give charitable donations? And on and on and on. All of these questions represent potential wisdom-producing situations. Each new day blesses us with additional opportunities to reflect, learn, and grow.

My Goodness: My Kids is a tribute to lay wisdom—parental lay wisdom. In it, I offer you the end product of 30 years of common-sense child rearing—theories and methods that worked to build character in my children. My kids are good, honest, steadfast, and courageous. They are my reward for taking on my child-rearing tasks with one eye on my immediate family and the other eye on the world around us. Now that my job is done, I have lots to share. I have stories of profound lessons learned—by my children and by me.

I expose my tools, including some unpopular methods and unconventional philosophies. I do this in the hope that you will be inspired to focus—first and foremost—on goodness and character building while you are raising your children. A generation of good children—who display honor and integrity in their daily lives—could minimize many of today's biggest problems: violence, cruelty, dishonesty, thievery, narcissism, exploitation, mistrust, substance abuse, arrogance, and more.

I have opened my family window so you can peek in. And now I am asking you to open yours. Please visit the "Coming Up" section at the back of this book to see how you can help build goodness and character in your children.

—NESTA AHARONI

INTRODUCTION

THE BEST WAY TO ELEVATE
THE MASSES IS TO RAISE
CHILDREN PROPERLY.

It's early, very early, on a weekend morning. It's tough to get up with an alarm on what traditionally is a lazy day. I hope I don't disturb my husband's sleep as I silently creep from my drowsy bedroom into my fluorescent writing retreat. Caffeine! That will help. That will jolt my brain cells into action.

As I sluggishly sip from my favorite coffee cup, I ask myself what in the world could be so important that I would sacrifice the comfort of my warm, cozy bed to sit in a straight-back chair at a rigid desk. Security is the answer. Security for individuals, for families, for the nation, and for the world.

In the shadows of an emerging morning, I realize that two events inspired me to sit at my plastic keyboard, contemplating the value of security. One, the ever-present, man-made evil that is depicted in the black ink of my morning newspaper, in the jarring sounds of my TV set, and in the disturbing news breaks of my radio programs. Two, the birth of my first grandchild.

In case you are now scratching your head, wondering how these two things could be related, I will take a moment to explain. It all starts with some friendly conversation.

I love talking with people. And I enjoy a great debate on the big issues of the day. But after ideas start to fly and opinions begin to express themselves, you can almost always hear me blurt out the following: "We could help prevent the heart-wrenching problems of cruelty and inhumanity if parents would dedicate themselves to raising 'good' children." When I say this, I don't mean successful, brilliant, or happy children. I mean "good" children—children who have strong character. Children who embody integrity, sympathy, kindness, and honesty. Children who have a value system that supports them. Children who care when others hurt, and whose contributions extend humbly beyond themselves.

So I sit here with my fingers itching to type, asking myself why I am qualified to write these pages—thoughts on how raising good children can contribute to making the world a better place. I am an ordinary, mainstream, run-of-the mill American wife, mother, worker, relative, and friend. I don't have a Ph.D. in human behavior. I am of average weight, height, and looks. I am blessed to have a kind-hearted husband, three honorable children, a mortgage, and a dog. But that is exactly why I feel I have something to share with you as our lives continue down their crisscross courses.

People often comment on my children's character and behavior. "It's luck," they say. Or "It's genetic." Others want to know how it happened that my children were always the designated driver rather than the drunk. How was it that my children never rebelled in ways that made their parents cringe? When so many other eager children were bursting to be first at the front of the line, why did my kids wait peacefully, confident that their turn would come? Why are my children willing to work so hard under an awe-inspiring work ethic? Why do they pursue justice under challenging circumstances when everyone else remains silent? Why would my children never dream of hurting another human being unless it became incumbent upon them to defend or protect?

These questions stimulated self-reflection: How did I raise three kids who have a conscience and radiate good character? I have never been a professional in the child-rearing field, but the proof is in the pudding. I did do it. I raised three good kids. I began to review my life and dig a little deeper. This book is the result of those efforts.

For 30 years I have been writing this work, but I never knew it. In fact, I couldn't even conceive of the task until all of my children turned 21 and convinced me—through their *actions*—that I had released three good kids into society. Now that I know it, I am ready to share in the hope that our family history can benefit others. So I invite you to take a peek at my musings, my uncertainties, and my realizations. I welcome you to peer through my family's window and see how I implemented my ideas, many of them unconventional and unpopular. As I introduce you to the inner workings of my family, I implore you to consider how you can instill goodness into your own children's character.

This book describes my thoughts, my memories, and my deeds. I am sitting in front of my computer early on a weekend morning with the hope that you can take something from my experiences and use it to cultivate a little humanity in a developing generation. I hope that together we can produce a safer, more secure world for my new grandchild and for all of the other people who share this planet with him.

BALANCE

ORDER IS NOT PRESSURE
THAT IS IMPOSED ON
SOCIETY FROM WITHOUT,
BUT AN EQUILIBRIUM
THAT IS SET UP FROM
WITHIN.
—JOSE ORTEGA Y GASSET

When we teach our children to live balanced lives, we prepare them for and protect them from the holes that will inevitably appear in their childhood playground. When two people sit on a seesaw, one goes up and the other goes down. Fun? Yes. But seesawing is more than entertainment. Seesawing teaches us that poise is necessary to maintain stability during years of wavering moments. Life is like a seesaw. If you concentrate only on the "ups," you will miss the thrills and rewards and lessons of the "downs." And if you concentrate only on the "downs," you will miss the excitement, motivation, and accomplishment of the "ups."

As a parent, I sometimes wobbled and fluttered precariously. But as I ascended and descended on my family's teeterboard, I realized the importance of teaching my children to maintain balance in their lives. By "balance," I meant living full and active lives that stimulated their intellect, inspired their creativity, fueled their physical activity, and aroused them to care about the needs of others. My children rode the family seesaw with me, and they learned its lessons. The balance they acquired while soaring to countless highs and plummeting to countless lows has enabled them to avoid many of life's depressing pitfalls. They now proceed ahead with steadiness and endurance.

Childhood and teenagehood are filled with ups and downs. Here are some examples parents might encounter. If a first love becomes your son's *life*, when she casts an eye at the new student in her P.E. class and tells your son goodbye, he feels alone—void of a life. If your child's *life* is reduced to finishing the 100-meter backstroke one second faster than the school record and she falls short of that goal, again, your child has no life. If your child's *life* is defined by being accepted into the school's popular group, but rejection is the reality, he feels isolated and forlorn. If your child's *life* has been defined by getting straight A's, but a B is clearly on the horizon, she feels like a failure. But if your child's *life* is replete with varied activities, when one thing doesn't work out, your youngster feels nothing more than a bump in the road—not total and dismal destruction.

I am not saying, "Children, do not have goals because you might get hurt." I am saying, "Children, have goals and work hard to achieve them. But if something leaves a hole in your childhood fabric, let other activities and interests fill the space."

And parents, this philosophy applies to you as well. My children never wanted to be the center of my existence. Filling their own needs as well as mine would have been too much pressure for them to deal with. They liked knowing that their hard knocks would not destroy me. I had a full life. If they were benched during a game or didn't get the lead in the school play, they always knew that mom was going to be just fine.

In my attempt to protect my children from feeling devastated when things fell short, I encouraged them, and even required them (with options), to be involved in a grab bag of activities. Yes, I sometimes insisted, but the introduction of choices within categories made the process easy. "Kids, for the sake of your health you need to be actively involved in a physical activity. Do you want it to be karate, soccer, swimming, track and field, or dance? Let me know." Or "Kids, for emotional health you need to be involved in something creative. Do you want it to be music lessons, theater, art, or voice training? Let me know."

Through their growing years, I stimulated the intellectual, creative, physical, social, and volunteer parts of my children's character. If one piece of their life's puzzle dealt them a blow, they had all of the other pieces to hold them together. Life was happening all around them—all of the time. One day was up and the next day was down. Each aspect of my children's lives, each activity they were involved in, helped them to focus on the totality of the ride rather than on the momentary setbacks. They learned to keep their axis strong and to maintain their equilibrium during uncertain times.

Introducing balance into my children's lives yielded fun and excitement for the entire family. We attended and enjoyed so many activities together: academic league competitions, swim team meets, water polo matches, air band rivalries, chamber choir concerts, theater performances, pole vaulting contests, piano recitals, show choir productions, concert presentations, fund-raising events, and more. My children enjoyed family celebrations, enduring friendships, school activities, spiritual training, outdoor endeavors, music, and the arts. One thing I learned from some very good teachers is that human beings are inherently multifaceted and complex—some days more so than others. The activities my children were involved in appealed to many different aspects of their personalities (like my middle child who is a singing, theater-performing, science-reading, pole vaulting, mountain unicyclist, who volunteers his time to his preferred causes). Through the comings and goings of the children, each member of the family felt uplifted and a little more fulfilled.

Yes, my children experienced inevitable losses in some areas of their lives—a lost meet, a bad fall, separation from a friend— but these hiccups didn't interrupt the flow of their lives, didn't cripple their performance, didn't depress their dispositions, didn't lead them to unhealthy and numbing alternative solutions.

After I became comfortable with my balance philosophy, a little voice in my head warned, "Don't overdo it. Don't burden your children with too many pursuits." So I extended my program over time. My children did not engage in all of the activities that interested them simultaneously. Certain activities, like music, were long term. Others, like karate lessons, were temporary, lasting a year or so. My goal was to ensure *full* lives—not crazy lives. My objective was to introduce my kids to *many* exciting things—not to insist that they become experts in any one of them.

After my children begged me to take on a new challenge, I insisted with full disclosure that they stick with the activity for a minimum of one year. At that point, if they decided to switch from piano to guitar, great. If they decided to switch from swimming to soccer, also great. This one-year time period gave my children the opportunity to get over the learning curve and determine if talent and/or passion were buried under the surface waiting to be discovered.

When each of my children started their first year of college, they were rewarded for the balance they had achieved. After reviewing their college course listings, they became stimulated, eager, and enthusiastic. They were so interested in so many things. They wanted to take just about every course that was offered. They learned how to narrow down their academic interests, create a plan, move towards a goal and, of course, balance their academic pursuits with physical exercise, friendship, meaningful conversation, community involvement, and plain old silliness and fun.

Moms and dads also teeter and totter as they work their way through the parental playground. But the best thing we can do for our children is to *balance our own lives*. Children do not and should not represent the entirety of their parents' lives. When my two oldest children left the house to pursue their aspirations, my third child was worried. The last thing she wanted was to be the focus of our existence. And she let us know that—loud and clear.

In addition to the time we devoted to our children, my husband and I filled in our own blanks. We expended energy on relationships, activities, and organizations that fulfilled us. We spent time together as a couple. Together we took dance lessons, joined couples' groups, went on dates, spent time with friends, and celebrated our relationship often. Individually, we went to the gym, learned artistic crafts, took classes, joined groups, and enjoyed the company of friends. We lived happy and fulfilling lives, and our children appreciated *not* being the center of our universe.

I decided to let my children waver and stagger—up and down, up and down. I supported them and offered advice, but I always maintained my own equilibrium. I let my stability and joy give them wings. They flew straight into the crosswinds, confronted life's challenges head on, made their own directional decisions, and solved their own problems. After all, it was, and still is, *their* journey to travel. Each one of my children had his or her own unique lessons to learn. I let their lessons be *their* lessons—not my lessons. I let their involvements enrich me but not become me. I let my engagement with life *stabilize* them but not overtake them. And I found, as a result, that we all were the better for it.

BOYS WILL BE BOYS

> MEN AND WOMEN BELONG
> TO A DIFFERENT SPECIES,
> AND COMMUNICATION
> BETWEEN THEM IS A
> SCIENCE STILL IN ITS
> INFANCY.
> —BILL COSBY

We appreciate males for being males in the animal kingdom. And we admire females for being females. But that view doesn't seem to carry through when we consider the human species. For quite a while now, a prevailing voice has been telling us that males and females are the same. And I agree—that men and women share equal competencies. I have a male friend who bakes cherry cheesecake and a female friend who fixes cars. But the modern world is pressing for gender sameness, suggesting that the sexes think the same, feel the same, and react the same. When I left school many years ago I shared that conviction, but raising three children has forced me to rethink the issue. Could it be that men and women really are different?

In the animal kingdom, we applaud distinction. When we observe a proud, powerful, fully horned bull in a field, we exclaim, "How magnificent!" We sense his strength in every rippling muscle. We feel his confidence as his head slowly rises to confront us. He sends us messages of self-assurance, strength, power, and ability. He heaves his burly body back and forth, eager to wrangle. He sweeps his legs impatiently in the dirt below him. He is in a state of readiness, and we see him as glorious.

And when we spy the beauty of a graceful doe enjoying a sunny, spring meadow with her newborns, we exclaim, "How delightful!" The lines of her willowy frame inspire us, as if she were a masterpiece created by nature's Pissarro. Her delicacy belies the fact that her eyes and ears are continuously sensing her surroundings. Her long, sleek muscles are constantly twitching in preparation of a swift and defensive departure. She is alert and capable. She is protective and nurturing. And we see her as stunning.

We value the roles the sexes play in diverse animal communities—fearless, roaming hunters contrasted with sheltering, domestic caretakers. We marvel at the differences in their exterior shells—peacocks decorated in a brilliant array of dazzling colors designed to attract the opposite sex, and peahens dressed in drab, colorless garb designed to protect themselves and their offspring. We understand the ancient magnetism that draws one sex to the other—male to female, female to male. Yet, when we consider our own species, the modern Western World leans toward androgyny.

We want everyone to be the same and to live in a homogenous unisex setting where men choose to shave their bodies (in an attempt to portray themselves as more sensitive), women choose *not* to shave their bodies (in an attempt to announce their gender equality), and girls carelessly engage in casual sex with a happy generation of young males (in an attempt to assert masculine power). Huge numbers of people are moving toward a gray, indistinguishable center.

In my college days, I supported the androgynous trend because that is what I was taught—we are the same. But having experienced decades of life with both sexes (a husband, two sons, and a daughter), I have outgrown that underdeveloped theory and discovered, through life experience, that the sexes, though of equal value and aptitude, are indeed different.

Yes, males can cook and help with homework while holding a crying baby. They excel as beauticians, teachers, librarians, and homemakers. And yes, females can build a bookcase, repair a dripping faucet, and manage the family finances. They shine as astronauts, soldiers, paramedics, and CEOs. Men can perform ballet, and women can play basketball. Physical and intellectual capabilities can be measured one individual at a time. But what about those mysterious, immeasurable qualities that fall under the umbrella of "masculinity" and "femininity"?

I learned about my family members' inherent masculine and feminine traits by colliding with them head on. I realized that even though my husband and sons desired to achieve psychological and emotional health (like my daughter and I did), the bulk of their energy, capabilities, and talent was expressed in external, problem-solving activities—swimming faster, jumping higher, and achieving educational or professional goals. The boys learned how to become men actively. They didn't whine when they came in second or third. They merely learned from their experiences and planned to improve the next time.

My daughter and I, on the other hand, have always been committed first and foremost to psychological, emotional, and spiritual development. It defines us. We spend time and effort on the endeavor and express it verbally. Like my husband and sons, my daughter and I expend energy on external goals, both educational and professional, but our proclivity is to spend time in the peaceful, quiet company of non-competitive trees.

Here are some examples I was confronted with as a parent. Eventually, they led me away from a theory of gender sameness and toward an understanding and celebration of gender differences.

I gave my young sons dolls and stuffed animals to play with in addition to trucks and cars. That's what we were told to do. These traditionally feminine toys were either neglected, taken apart, or used as battering rams. They weren't fast enough, loud enough, or destructive enough to keep the boys' interest. The boys *preferred* things that moved (the faster, the better) and went "zoom" (the louder, the better), and things they could take apart (the quicker, the better). They did not nurture their toys. They crashed their toys. There was no emotional attachment there.

I gave my young daughter trains and planes to play with in addition to dolls and tea sets. These traditionally masculine toys were neglected, but never disassembled or crashed. They weren't cute enough or cuddly enough to keep her interest. She *preferred* soft, squishy stuffed animals she could cram into her pajamas at night, and books that lived to become dear friends. She connected to her toys. They became her companions and confidants. There was lots of emotional attachment there.

My boys always wanted to wear oversized T-shirts with knee-length shorts and sturdy, high-topped shoes. Minor changes took place as they grew into high school students. The Batman on the front of the elementary school T-shirt evolved into an Escher work of art at the high school level. The shoes that were black and white in elementary school evolved into a rainbow of metallic delights. Dressing up was tolerated as a sign of respect at weddings, bar mitzvahs, graduations, and funerals. Hairstyles changed according to current standards: short crop, medium crop, ponytail, and the wave. But basically, when on their own time, what the boys wore then is what the boys wear now. Fashion did not dictate their choices. Comfort did—and still does. They preferred to announce who they were through actions and deeds. Very logical, indeed.

My daughter delighted in creating her own fashion style. As she humored me through elementary school by wearing cute little outfits I matched for her, she was patiently planning her coming-out strategy: to find a style that expressed who she was and how she was unique. This was a process, with one fashion change following another. The outfits she wears today—long, flowing skirts and exotic sarongs (that complement each other but don't match, God forbid)—are far from her elementary school existence. Her style has evolved. She has made herself over many times. The process is what was important to her: to feel it, to ponder it, to experiment with it, to grow from it. Very transforming indeed.

When my sons had a problem with another boy, it was *usually* wrestled away, tether-balled away, or settled with a slap on the back. Confrontation was honest, out in the open, and swift. Normally, grudges were not held. The boys' goal was to get back into play as quickly as possible. (Softer reactions, such as excommunication, did exist, but they were not the rule. And though the bulk of reactions were indeed physical, full-blown fights were a last resort.) Issues were evident and accessible.

When my daughter had a problem with another girl, it was *usually* unspoken and underground. Other girls in the friendship circle were consulted. Manipulations commenced. Gossip raged. Hurt feelings mounted. Tears were shed. Damage was done. Issues were hidden and rarely confronted head on.

My boys loved bicycles, skateboards, and competition. They wanted to feel the wind on their faces and the air (or water) under their feet. One went from the discipline of a medal-driven swim team to the wild and wooly antics of water polo. The other went from pole vaulting to unicyling to mountain unicycling (when ordinary street unicycling became too tame.) Athletic competition, against others and against their own past performances, was important to them. Ribbons, medals, and varsity jackets adorned their rooms.

When my daughter was old enough to graduate from a tricycle to a bicycle, she fell down once (despite her dad's running effort to keep her up) and decided that was enough of that. In fairness to her, 15 years later, when it was *her* idea, she got back on a bike and is now pedaling to her heart's content. I have no memories of her on a skateboard—ever. During P.E. class, she would wait in a long line of kids, most of whom were eager to kick the ball. Before she approached the front of the line, she inevitably snuck to the back—without ever having touched the target. But she *loved* to perform in show choirs—dancing, singing, and playing piano to the delight of her audiences.

Awards were inconsequential to her, building her talent and her confidence was.

When my boys got together with their friends, they jumped, climbed, ran, tossed, and banged. When my daughter got together with her friends, they talked, colored, created, role-played, and taught.

When my young boys went to the doctor's office to get a shot, they bravely watched the antiseptic proceedings. Needle pricks were insignificant to them when compared to the bumps, scrapes, gashes, breaks, and bruises that usually adorned them. When my little daughter went to the doctor's office, she expressed her fears. It took the entire nursing staff to hold her down. Her shoes flew ceiling high. Her screams were deafening.

As I began to notice differences between the sexes, one idea remained solid: Capabilities and talents were gender neutral in our family. I have one son who is passionate about dancing, theatre, and music. I have another son who enjoys cooking, singing, and *The Canterbury Tales*. I have a daughter who braves monster roller coasters and can hike all summer in tough mountain terrain carrying 50 pounds on her back. I am not a traditionalist when it comes to activities and competencies. But I have become a traditionalist when it comes to inherent masculine and feminine inclinations.

As my child-rearing years progressed and the evidence grew, I learned to let boys be boys and girls be girls. I simply let each child be who he or she naturally was. The lesson for me was to let my children's instinctive proclivities emerge. Let my boys crash their toy cars in giant, head-on collisions. Let my daughter hug her stuffed rabbit with tenderness and care. I learned to honor who they were and not to fashion them into a modern trend.

As I philosophized about natural inclinations, I realized the beauty of the masculine-feminine design. *We need each other.* Often, males need females to teach them about gentleness, compassion, and intimacy (among other things). And often, females need males to teach them about logic, practicality, and building an empire (among other things). Getting the sexes to get along is a tremendous challenge, but maybe *that is the point.*

Now that the children are adults, I notice the theme continuing. My boys usually call me to share information about recent accomplishments. My daughter usually calls me to talk about her feelings. That does not mean that my boys are oblivious to emotions and my daughter is disinterested in success. All of my children are concerned with all of these things, but *it is their natural inclinations I am talking about.* My boys are comfortable in their masculine skin (even if they are cooking and cleaning). And my daughter is comfortable in her feminine mind-set (even if she is performing home repairs). My children are not conflicted about their identities. This self-assurance helps them to be happy and tranquil, two qualities that, if adopted by others, could help contribute to a more peaceful world.

CHORES AND ALLOWANCE

THE ALLOWANCES YOU
GIVE YOUR CHILDREN
NEVER DO AS MUCH HARM
AS THE ALLOWANCES YOU
MAKE FOR THEM.

As I struggled with the concept
of uniting kids with household chores and an allowance, my
mind took me on a journey to my youth. Maybe I could find an
answer there to the following questions: Should my children be
responsible for regular chores? If so, how many and how often?
Should they be rewarded with an allowance for contributing
to the maintenance of the household? While reminiscing, I
remembered something definite about the childhood chores I
was forced to complete. I didn't like them. Yet there were other
tasks around the house that I did enjoy and volunteered for—
like helping my mother in the kitchen while she was preparing
dinner. Kitchen time was memorable—many precious mother-
daughter moments chopping, slicing, stirring, mincing, and
learning how to feed a family of five.

Here is what I remembered about receiving an allowance:
I felt my weekly allowance was not commensurate with the
amount of work I did. I know what house cleaners are paid

today to scrub other people's toilets and vacuum their carpets, and it is a whole lot more than a quarter a week. I understand that I received a roof over my head, plenty of food to eat, and a constant flow of parental love. But the regular stipend I received was only enough to purchase a Look bar, some Necco's, and some red wax lips. It was not enough to teach me how to budget and save for more significant purchases.

Children have a responsibility to their family. It is character-building for them to pitch in and help out. After all, a family moves forward as a group *and* as discrete units. I pondered how I could teach my children the concepts of contribution and obligation without having to suppress weekly chore rebellions or demean their efforts with a paltry bit of change. I thought about how I could bring accountability—and even joy—into the equation. I did not want to create an environment in which chipping in meant dragging feet and surly moods.

I decided to turn my children into family rescuers. The basic rule was this: Kids, your job is to focus on your schoolwork and your activities—because they will get you farther in life than polishing the silverware or dusting the living room furniture—yet again. But when the family needs your help, I expect you to be there and to jump in, without complaint. And that's exactly how it went.

The upkeep of our family home was generally mom and dad's responsibility. After all, we made the decision to have a house of a particular size with a yard of particular dimensions and a dog of a particular shape and temperament. But the children were enjoying the consequences of our decision making, so they also needed to become active partners. Although their involvement didn't entail regular chores on a weekly basis (other than tidying their rooms now and then), it did include lending a hand (or two) when needed—after the last pages of homework were completed, after club meetings were attended, and after sports training and events were concluded. I never asked my children to stay up late and lose precious sleep in order to carry out a household chore. It was more important to me that they be rested and able to fulfill the responsibilities of school and related activities because *school and its related activities were their job*—a job I expected them to take seriously.

Here's how it unfolded:

My husband and I performed household maintenance tasks. And the kids were there, when needed. They helped with heavy lifting, assisted in equipment repairs, pushed disobedient cars, and packed trash bags with the brown-and-green residue of yard work.

When I was expecting company for a holiday dinner party, the kids were there to help. They set tables (in some very unique and creative ways), chopped vegetables, served soup, cleared away the mess, and washed or dried the dishes. And they enjoyed it because instead of being forced, they felt they were pitching in. They were part of the family party team.

When overnight guests came to visit, the kids were on it— making beds, straightening up their rooms, and cleaning up the bathroom.

Over time, an interesting development occurred. I discovered that certain children were naturally attracted to certain chores. After I figured this out, I was able to request their help with tasks that they actually enjoyed. This made the recruitment process much easier. "Sure, Mom, I'll help wash the dog."

One child loved being in the kitchen chopping vegetables and stirring pots. While his competent hands were moving gracefully in slicing and swirling patterns, his mind was sorting through a hard drive of impressive ideas. As ingredients were thrown into the bottom of the Dutch oven, his thoughts rose to the surface and became fascinating topics of conversation— which made our shared culinary activities interesting and enjoyable. Today, ideas and concepts are his business. Maybe some of those skills were developed in our humble family kitchen.

Another child regularly and consistently made his bed and straightened his room. He had no interest in what was going on in the kitchen—other than devouring the end product. But his bed was made and his room was neat (to a certain extent), every single day. His devotion to order served him well as he contemplated, planned, and executed his life's plan. Today, order and preparation define him. His ducks are always lined up neatly in a row.

Another child loved setting tables and doing dishes. If company was coming for dinner, you could guarantee that the table was adorned with candles, flowers, colors, and patterns. In addition, she was adept at scrubbing dishes until they were spotless. She enjoyed catching bubbles that floated above the sink and soaking her hands in the warmth of soapy water. She was fast and adept then and is fast and adept now. She still finds ways to bring joy and balance to a life weighted with many educational responsibilities.

I could have forced my children regularly to scrub a floor that didn't look dirty or polish some furniture that already glowed, but they wouldn't have seen the point. By engaging their energy and ability at strategic times, when I needed them the most, they were able to feel that they were helping out the family and contributing to something concrete and measurable, something that clearly needed to be accomplished. At these times, they felt important and vital. They prided themselves on the fact that they could help dad lift a heavy mattress and the frame of a newly purchased bed. Or that they could clean and set up 40 chairs in preparation for an upcoming get-together. They enjoyed the compliments that flowed as mom and dad described to guests how they helped create a beautiful dining room table or a delicious pot of homemade soup.

In our house, helping family members when they needed it was not rewarded with money. Help was given out of a sense of responsibility to the family unit. We supported each other by lending our hands and exerting our energy. We contributed to the advancement of each person and to the success of the group.

But what about purchases? How did the kids buy things? Well, when it came to clothing, haircuts, school supplies, etcetera, they got what they needed and what we could afford. That meant no designer labels, no $100 tennis shoes, and no fancy backpacks. With that understood, we had fun shopping around town and finding items we all could live with.

If there was a particular something someone wanted that was priced above and beyond what mom and dad were willing to invest in it, that child had the opportunity to work for it. Often the kids ran up to me begging," Mom, do you have any jobs that need to be done around the house?" This was a great time for my husband and me to check household projects off of our to-do list. I remember my poor daughter spending days on her hands and knees cleaning the grout on the kitchen floor with a bottle of bleach and a toothbrush. But she was happy to do it and to *earn* her reward. She never complained. She blasted her music and sang her way through the backbreaking mission.

Today, I have one grown child who prefers to do her clothes shopping at thrift stores. In these low-priced establishments, she comes across many good-quality products. She mixes and matches from a variety of styles in order to create her fashion personality. She shuns the more expensive stores in favor of practicality. I have another child who has decided to own as few tangible items as possible. He prefers a life free of the constraints and entanglements of unnecessary things. And I have yet another child who enjoys the benefits of a good sound system, but he has the patience to work for it and to save for it. Music never sounded so good.

My children learned the value of a dollar. They know how to live within a budget and to work hard for luxury items. We didn't offer weekly chores to them or pitiful allowances, but we did build a network of family cooperation and collaboration.

The things my children felt intrinsically drawn to do back then are the same things they are attracted to today. Those who loved neat beds back then, love neat beds today. Those who enjoyed making guacamole back then, enjoy making guacamole today. Those who took pleasure setting a dinner table back then, take pleasure in setting a dinner table today. And those who were fond of slicing carrots back then, are fond of slicing carrots today.

Maybe my lesson is a lesson other parents can benefit from: *Let your children gravitate toward the duties that they are naturally inclined to perform.* When I followed my children's lead and encouraged them to take on assignments willingly, I enabled them to fashion their own rewards. They participated in something they enjoyed doing. They shared a conflict-free environment with their parents. And they prided themselves on a job well done. Meanwhile, I was able to rest easy knowing that my children were developing a sense of responsibility to the family, a willingness to contribute, and an understanding of the value of their cooperation.

CONSISTENCY

ALWAYS REMEMBER THAT
YOUR OWN RESOLUTION
TO SUCCEED IS MORE
IMPORTANT THAN
ANYTHING ELSE.
—ABRAHAM LINCOLN

To parents, consistency means applying the same principles and course of action repeatedly and unfailingly in order to achieve the behavior results they want. Consistency in child rearing is critical. When it is present, it teaches your children that you mean what you say and that testing you is a waste of their time and energy. When it is absent, it teaches your children that you can be ignored and manipulated.

I have repeatedly witnessed the following scenario in other families: a child out of control at a friendly gathering or in a supermarket. A mom or dad shouts, "Stop that." The son or daughter actually stops *for a nanosecond*, after which the darling continues the offending behavior.

When my first child was an infant, I struggled to find a solution to the defiant attitude I knew was sure to come. So many kids were not taking their parents seriously. Was there a way out of the uncomfortable public displays being acted out all around me? Was the ignore-mom-and-dad behavior inevitable? As I watched the family dynamics of others playing out, I came up with a strategy that turned out to be remarkably simple and commonsensible—but it was also demanding, challenging, and easier said than done. Consistency, I decided, would be my plan and my solution.

Let me take you on a visual of my newfound approach. Imagine that I am at a party or get-together. The cheerful group of people I am socializing with may be celebrating a holiday, a birthday, or an anniversary. I am engrossed in conversation. It could be focused on anything, from global politics to the differences between men and women. I am joyful and animated as I share my thoughts and absorb the words of others. Discussion and laughter are the theme of the day. In short, I am socially engaged and having a wonderful time.

With an intuitive sense I turn my head. I feel something indefinable break my concentration. What do I see? My little toddler pulling healthy, sea-green leaves off of our hosts' favorite outdoor plant. *Or* feeding their beloved dog, Bowser, a piece of chocolate birthday cake. *Or* creating a vibrant, multicolored crayon masterpiece on our hosts' freshly painted fence. The options are endless.

Now comes the hard part. I have to act. And even though it is not easy to do—it is imperative. I must stop *whatever I am doing*—no matter how much I am enjoying doing it. It is imperative that I break my concentration and absorption. I am obligated to my hosts and my child to put down my plate, which happens to be heaped with barbequed flank steak, a buttery baked potato, and everyone's favorite side—the unnamed, cherry pink, cottage cheesy, Jell-O-ey delight. I love food and conversation, but my devotion to those things must now take a backseat role. It is essential that I pull myself up from my chair—no matter how reluctant I am to do so—enter my child's space and take care of business—swiftly and *consistently*.

I don't like the interruption. I would much rather be partaking in the conversation and companionship of friends and family members—or in the mile-high mountain that is heaped on my super-sized plate. But the day I decided to have children was the day I dedicated myself to raising and then releasing into society individuals who would be assets, not liabilities. So I remind myself of this annoying fact, and I get up and act like a committed parent should.

Now that I am out of my chair, how am I going to stop the offending behavior—this time and *each and every time it happens?* The approach I settled on was this: Take that little leaf-pulling hand in mine. Squeeze it gently, but firmly. Look directly into my child's eyes and talk to him—briefly but to the point—about consequences. Talk about how a plant "feels" when its display of leaves is ripped from its core one by one. Or talk about how the hosts feel when they see that something that was once so healthy and beautiful is now a graveyard of empty stems. Talk about Bowser and how chocolate cake—even though delightful and delicious—can cause chaos and confusion in his little doggy stomach. Talk about the protective, sturdy fence and how much effort was involved in coating it with just the perfect blush of redwood. Talk about whatever comes to mind, a sentence or two that expresses what is wrong and *who is being affected.* By making physical contact (holding my child's hand firmly), communicating directly (looking straight into his eyes), and using words to express the effects of my child's actions, I intended to make the point that I was serious.

Okay. Finished. I did my duty. Where is my plate of pink cottage-cheesy stuff? And where were we in our discussion of coed dormitories for college students? I am settled back in with adult companions. I am eating. I am talking. I am listening. Life is good.

Oh, no! There it is again. That intuitive tap on the shoulder directing me to turn my head. Again, I force myself to break my concentration, and again I see the need to act. My child has resumed his leaf-pulling, dog-feeding, picture-drawing behavior.

Reluctantly, I pull myself up from my chair—again. The

plate of food I was relishing takes its place on my seat—again. I don't want to get up a second time. I am enjoying myself. But I owe it to my family, my hosts, *and to society* to do so. I repeat my process—holding the miniature hand, staring into the big eyes, and explaining the effects of certain behaviors. But this time, I see a glimmer of hope. His toddler brain is getting it. He understands that the plant's loveliness is on display. He comprehends that an act of generosity can cause pain to a canine creature. He appreciates the effort that was exerted to beautify the fence, the backyard, and the party space. I am feeling positive. I may be able to finish my meal yet.

My prediction was right. The behavior stopped. It stopped for one reason and one reason only. I forced myself up and out of my chair to deal with my parental duties—*each and every time* my toddler acted. Consistency is the key to shaping a child's behavior. Other families taught me that my kids would never take me seriously as a parent, or respect me, if I reprimanded them lazily or selfishly and without follow-through. My system was simple. It was sensible. It was difficult. It was demanding. But the rewards proved to be great.

But what if my plan hadn't worked? What if my child didn't stop screaming, demanding, or misbehaving at a party, in a restaurant, or at the grocery. (And that certainly did happen.) What should my next step be? How would I send the message that I am a strong parent who will not be ignored or manipulated? Should I just buy him the chocolate bar displayed at the checkout counter in order to keep him quiet and avoid embarrassment—even though I don't want him to have it? No. Instead, I reverted to Plan B.

Plan B was to remove the offending child—kicking or screaming or crying—from whatever environment we were in. I would simply pick him up and take him out—away from stimulation and other people. If that meant leaving my loaded grocery cart, so be it. If that meant walking out of a cozy restaurant, so be it. If that meant separating from other party guests, so be it. My child was going to learn to earn his way back into society without annoying, ignoring, or manipulating others. Plan B achieved two goals: One, punishment. If he didn't stop the disagreeable behavior, he would not be allowed to continue enjoying his surroundings. Two, respect—for the other people in the area who were certain to become irritated by the sight and sounds of a challenging child.

How do moms and dads choose their parental battles? How do they decide whether to take one behavior on and let another one slide? For me, the criterion was this: Are other people affected by the behavior, or is the action something personal that affects only me and my child? Having a full-blown tantrum in the middle of Macy's affects other shoppers and employees. I would feel compelled to stop misbehavior in that setting— consistently. But if my child stretched out his curious hand to enjoy the texture of a fuzzy fabric and knocked five sweaters to the floor, I would understand. We would simply pick up the clothing items, replace them neatly on the rack, and move on.

I never made visible displays of my consistency actions, explanations, or removals. How could I teach my children to respect other people and their things if I did not show them respect publicly? Explanations were made privately and quietly, and removals were made swiftly and good-naturedly. My intent was not to embarrass or humiliate my children. It was to achieve a goal: a smooth interface between my offspring and the rest of society.

The older my children grew, the more I was able to fully enjoy guests, parties, discussions, celebrations, and mealtimes. I still witnessed children causing their unique brand of disruption and damage. But now *I could stay in my chair*. Why? Because they were not *my* children.

My children learned when they were young that seeing mom rise out of her chair once was more than enough. And hearing mom explain the effects of their behavior once was more than enough. They knew that if they didn't get it the first time, mom would be back—over and over and over again—insisting on her desired result. Mom meant what she said.

My children also learned the importance of respecting other people's time, space, and things. And eventually they chose to do so—*on their own*. Because I confronted misbehavior head on when my children were young, during toddler and preschool years, I was able to enjoy myself regularly when they were older. They benefited from the plan I implemented. I benefited from the plan I implemented. Everyone around us benefited from the plan. And all because of one little word—consistency—which, I heartily admit, is easier said than done.

DINNERTIME CONVERSATION

CONVERSATION IS THE
ART OF HEARING AS WELL
AS BEING HEARD
—William Hazlitt

Dinnertime can be a gift to parents who are eager to communicate with their children and help them develop crucial mental skills: how to think through an idea, how to struggle with a concept, how to present and defend a point of view, how to handle constructive criticism, and how to accept opposing positions gracefully.

I remember dinnertime with my family when I was growing up in Los Angeles. But it's hard to recall those evening gatherings without having the urge to put on some protective gear and develop aggressive instincts. Dinnertime at my parents' home was war—over who was going to get the biggest and best piece of chicken (or beef or enchilada). I remember my family members flying out of their seats—leaning forward, grabbing, and then guarding their catch. Elbows soared as dishes flashed before my eyes. The conversation was limited to "Hey, you took too much" or "That's the piece I wanted" or "Get your fingers out of the mashed potatoes." While this cutthroat environment may have been good training for one day entering a competitive workforce, it didn't teach me much of anything else.

When I was raising my own family, I decided to abandon the aerobic dinnertime exercises I had been exposed to. Dinnertime became a time of sharing *civilly*—not just events of the day, but challenging ideas as well. Family members volunteered to come up with topics of discussion. The kids loved to present thought-provoking issues. Sometimes the chosen subject was inspired by something they had learned from a teacher or a friend. Other times, the kids were eager to thrash out ideas that had been presented in a movie, a book, or a TV show. Other themes developed from deep reflection—the magical musings kids engage in late at night when they are sheltered in a dark and silent room contemplating the wonders of the universe and the meaning of it all.

Many of our discussions were centered on ethical themes— what's right and what's wrong. Would you cheat on an application to get into the college of your choice? What are you giving up when you make a decision to deceive? How about underage drinking, designated drivers, and loyalty to friends? Should you notify parents of their children's out-of-control behavior? How about a conversation about marijuana? Do people who use this drug relax their ambitions and their willingness to reach goals they once eagerly embraced? Does using marijuana lead to harder drug use? Does the human body become satisfied with one level of stimulation, or is it insatiable—always demanding more? What about handing out condoms on campuses? Does that encourage early sexual behavior? Or should we adopt this attitude: "They are going to do it anyway, so we might as well make sure that they are healthy and pregnancy free?"

Then there were all of those philosophical and theological questions? Why does one child hurt, embarrass, or bully another? Must I show respect to my classroom teacher if he or she is not showing respect to the students? Do I speak up if a teacher is humiliating another student publicly? What is the explanation for human evil? How do certain cruel people become powerful political leaders? Is there a God who created the universe? What about scientific theories like the Big Bang? If there is a God, does he actively care about us, or does he merely observe our behavior?

And on and on and on. These dinnertime conversations ignited sparks in my children. They learned to love the process of formulating ideas, defending them, and accepting input from other family members. They discovered that good people don't always agree—but that's okay. They realized that there isn't always the contrast of a black-and-white, right-or-wrong solution, and that shades of gray pervade many issues. They understood the value of an open mind. If they thought they had unraveled a universal mystery, they soon recognized that two other people around the table held opposing points of view. During those conversations, they had to consider: Do I stick to my guns? Do I adopt my brother's point of view? Do I weaken myself if I accept a compromise?

Compromise was a skill that was mastered at our dinner table. Can I move a little toward the center from my extreme point of view? And if I do, will my guiding principle become stronger or weaker? Does compromise make me more or less powerful? My children were able to reduce potential upset in our home by knowing how to compromise—on money, designer labels, nights out, and homework time. As a result, they are now able to decrease the level of upset in their adult worlds. They work respectfully and cooperatively with professors, employers, spouses, friends, and relatives.

The key word here is "respect." By "respect" I mean the esteem or regard one person holds for another. Respect for other family members was the medium through which our ideas flowed. Respect enabled us to struggle with newly presented concepts without destroying the messenger. Respect at the dinner table was not the "end." It was the "means" that enabled us to tackle our topics enthusiastically and considerately.

What were my parental options if civility was not displayed? One, I could have brought the stimulating conversation to an abrupt halt. Two, I could have asked the person who crossed the line to leave the table. Since I can't remember ever ending a conversation prematurely or banning someone from the dinner table, I have to surmise that my husband's and my courteous and accepting behavior set a standard that was accepted by my children.

As ideas, instead of elbows, flew around our dinner table, we learned to display the flexible fabric of an open mind, not the rigid shield of resistance. We were careful to communicate respectfully, in deference to the person who was presenting a point of view. Why were we so careful? Because each one of us knew that soon it was going to be our turn to speak, and we too wished to be shown consideration. No opinion was too silly to present, but you had to be prepared to defend yourself. If you couldn't, someone was going to uncover—politely and enthusiastically—the flaws in your argument.

It was important for the kids to learn that if someone criticizes your position, it is not a criticism of you. The space around our dinner table was a safe environment. The kids felt free to stretch beyond the fence posts of their current consciousness. An idea might be rejected, but a person never was. As a result, many creative ideas were offered just for the sake of argument. Sometimes the children suggested a peculiar proposition just to get everyone's energy flowing. When they threw an imaginative idea onto the table, this food-for-thought was grabbed at, tossed around, and either digested or spit out. It was the *process* that was important to the kids—listening, examining, comprehending, and formulating responses. In the end, we could accept or reject the ideas that were presented. That was each person's personal decision.

A bonus factor slowly ripened for me over time. As my children grew from elementary school students into high school students, they learned to challenge me—considerately and courteously—but often relentlessly. What a gift! I remember smiling inwardly as my children tested me to see if I could back up a stated point of view. If they couldn't go out on a weeknight, they wanted to know why. If their homework was done and they were caught up with their responsibilities, what was damaged? So I grew—as a parent and as a thinker. I learned to formulate reasons quickly and to offer multilayered directives.

The beauty of the dinner table training was that my children became comfortable attempting to coerce me. But once a law was signed, sealed, and delivered, it was accepted by them without tantrums, foul language, or loss of confidence. In fact, I remember seeing their smiles when I finished a conversation with, "That was well done. You presented some great arguments. Nice try. But. . . . " This particular approach takes strength and compromise on the part of the parents. For me, a "because-I-said-so" response might have been easier, but addressing the challenges my children presented was more fun, stimulating, and thought provoking.

It takes confidence to challenge an authority figure. And our children were given the environment they needed to question, yet respect. To argue, yet accept. To stand firm, yet negotiate. What wonderful skills to carry one day into their own nuclear families and into the workplace.

I know my children enjoyed and were invigorated by these mental boot camp exercises. How do I know? They continue to engage in them today. When the kids come to visit my husband and me and we sit around the dinner table to share a meal, inevitably one of them eagerly asks, "Okay. What is the topic for today? I have a good one to offer."

In fact, years ago one of my sons described on a college application that he was inspired to think deeply and clearly by a little group of five family members who sat around a simple, aged dining room table tossing around ideas.

Stimulating conversation at dinnertime tightened our family bonds. We became closer as we grew to understand the workings of each others' minds. We appreciated this person's reticence on one particular issue, and that person's boldness on another. We helped each other see alternate points of view, and we honored each person's final decisions. Dinnertime was a time to be together as a family, sharing our day's experiences and communicating interesting concepts.

EMPATHY

COMPASSION IS THE BASIS
OF ALL MORALITY.
−Arthur Schopenhauer

Empathy is one of the most important character traits parents can cultivate in their children. Empathy is an understanding and emotional attachment to the feelings of others. How can children interact in the world in a compassionate, controlled, and gentle way without embracing this trait? Empathy enables children to relate to the feelings, situations, and motives of others and to emotionally attach.

An empathetic person is the opposite of a psychopath. Psychopaths are often adept at using an *emotionally free* understanding of others against them. How can we, as parents, teach our children that they are important, but that their feelings are not the center of the universe? How can we let them know that every other person in their circle of contacts is also consequential—including mom, dad, sister, and brother? How can we teach our children that other people feel pain, anger, frustration, and hurt? Empathy is one of many factors that can prevent one child from hurting another—physically, emotionally, or mentally. Without empathy, a me-first attitude has room to grow, and this can lead to only-I-am-right and only-I-am-deserving behaviors.

The world is filled with examples of everyday selfish behavior. When a child snubs an enduring friendship in order to be accepted into a new and popular group, he or she is lacking empathy and causing pain. The fact that a cherished friend is suffering rejection and loneliness is far less important to the status seeker than their desire to be part of the "in" group. When one child humiliates another publicly in order to feel superior, again, he or she is lacking empathy and causing pain. The embarrassed victim wants nothing more than to dig a hole and hide.

The Columbine shooters took a lack of empathy to the extreme. They delighted in verbally tormenting their victims before they shot them. Were they capable of emotionally attaching to the feelings of the trembling teenagers they were about to destroy? Did they have the capacity to feel sympathy for the plight of their prey? Were they able to feel their victims' terror? If those shooters were capable of feeling empathy for their fellow students, could they have pulled the trigger—again and again?

As I ruminated over and grappled with my own child-rearing issues, I realized that instilling kindness in my kids early on was an important part of raising good children. I understood the coin toss involved here. Many good parents despaired over bad-seed offspring. And I recognized that there was more to the goodness story than parenting alone. After all, many children who suffered terrifying abuse grew up to become kind and compassionate adults. But I acknowledged that there were things I could do to help shape a self-centered toddler into an empathetic child, adolescent, and adult.

Many years ago I took my first step toward instilling empathy in my children—but I was not even aware that I was doing it. I chose a kind marriage partner. I married a caring man who was capable of acting as a strong role model and parenting partner.

After I made that preliminary decision, the kids started to arrive. As the house filled up, I gradually developed a strategy that would help my husband and me send considerate and kind-hearted playmates onto the playground.

To illustrate how my empathy-building strategy worked, let me invite you to a restaurant. Almost all parents have endured annoyed looks and agitated gestures when their precious little angels misbehaved, screamed, demanded, and talked back in public eateries. I was not immune. It happened to me, too.

When my children were too young either to know better or control themselves, I simply took them outside to calm down. This mother-child exit allowed me to respect the needs of the other restaurant patrons (role modeling) and to quietly engage my fussy child one-on-one (parenting). Even though the kids were just babies and not yet able to understand my words or respond to my efforts, I gently talked to them about the peace and harmony restaurant goers desire when they journey out of their homes to enjoy a meal. I could feel my kids' bodies soften and relax as I gently whispered soothing sounds into their ears. Sometimes I would follow my explanation with some humming or lyrics. The individual attention I gave my children, beyond the busy restaurant environment, worked wonders.

When the children grew older and were able to comprehend my message, I became more creative. To illustrate this point, let's try another restaurant. This one is pleasantly decorated and dimly lit. My family members and I are seated at a comfortable booth enjoying superb spices and service. The restaurant staff is polite and charming. Quiet conversation is taking place all around us. Mature couples, developing relationships, and long-time friends are all sharing a well-deserved evening out. Suddenly the peace is broken by the loud, piercing voice of one of mine. What to do? What to do? How do I control this situation without creating more public disturbance?

Here is what I came up with—*and it always worked!* I looked gently into the eyes of my offending child. I pointed to another table, and then I made up a story.

I might have whispered to my child something like this: "See that couple over there? I think they have been dating and are falling in love. Maybe tonight is a special night. Maybe tonight he is going to ask her to marry him."

As I spoke in a quiet and soothing voice, my child's eyes got bigger and bigger. He felt as if he had been included in a special secret.

I added, "A loud noise now could break the romantic spell around their table. A loud voice now could interrupt their future plans."

The end result of this story, and others like it, *always* was that my once-noisy child decided to work ceaselessly the rest of the meal to ensure undisturbed tranquility for the other restaurant patrons. My child decided *on his own* to talk quietly—with absolutely no resentment on his part.

Here is another story: "See that couple over there. I think their day was very, very difficult. I think they worked too hard, and they are tired and worried. I think they came to this restaurant to relax and regroup."

Again, the big eyes. Again, a special secret. Again, my child worked ceaselessly to ensure that this deserving couple found the stillness they were seeking—with absolutely no defensiveness on his part.

I never told my children to "be quiet." I merely set up a scenario and let them make the decision on their own. I illustrated to them how their actions affected others. And I did it without having to suffer through a loud and antagonistic response. I never had to appear harsh and authoritarian in a public setting. By using this system, I was able to build a more lasting result. Each story brought me a step closer to building empathy in my children. Once they understood two principles—1) other people have feelings, too, and 2) your actions affect those around you—it was not long before they began making the decision to behave well on their own.

Today, my kids tell me that in addition to the story-telling approach, my husband and I role modeled empathy for them. Incidents related to them about friends, family, and acquaintances were critical to the development of their empathetic personalities. Because of their recent feedback, I feel comfortable telling you that every time you visit someone in the hospital, cook for someone who is ill, invite someone who is down on their luck, cheer someone who is sad, listen to someone who is lonely, calm someone who is upset, celebrate with someone who is joyful, take someone to a doctor's appointment, water your neighbor's plants, volunteer at the local school, or help in the community, you are building empathy in your children. For this, you need no strategy, no plan, and no struggle. *You simply need to be a decent person.*

Children benefit and respond when their parents understand and share the feelings of others. Just as my children watched me, your children are watching you. The decision you make today to react kindly to a particular person or gently in a specific situation can encourage the development of empathy in your child's character.

"EVERYBODY'S DOING IT"/ INDIVIDUALITY

NO BIRD SOARS TOO HIGH
IF HE SOARS WITH HIS
OWN WINGS.
—WILLIAM BLAKE

"But Mom, everybody's doing it."

"So if everybody jumped off a bridge, would you do that too?"

Children make the "everybody's-doing-it" gripe with conviction, as if the fact that everyone is doing *it* is proof that *it* cannot possibly be wrong. As a neophyte parent struggling with child-rearing ideas, how was I going to arm myself against the inevitable everybody's-doing-it attack?

My first thought was to teach my young children foundational values that were right or wrong, black or white. Like every other parent, I hoped my children wouldn't lie, cheat, or steal—and that they would judge those behaviors in others as wrong. But I knew there would be less obvious issues to confront, like whom to invite (or not invite) to a birthday party or whether to tell a friend's parents if he or she is behaving badly. After my children understood certain black-and-white basics—like not talking about someone behind their back; not engaging in manipulative lies to friends, parents, or teachers; not taking a piece of candy that you didn't pay for; and not cheating on a test—we could then proceed to the gray areas case by case.

Next, I wanted to encourage my children to engage in a variety of stimulating and fulfilling activities. If their minds and bodies were busy, motivated, and inspired with creative projects and physical challenges, they would care much less about who was wearing what to school and which CD other kids were listening to.

Finally, I decided to influence my children to be courageous enough to develop into individuals who could make decisions (*not* to drink that beer, *not* to smoke that joint, *not* to skip that class, *not* to kiss that boy) and generate ideas that drifted outside the general tide. Individualistic thinkers have the opportunity to contribute in big ways. Would Einstein have discovered the theory of relativity if he thought and behaved like everyone else? Were vaccines discovered by people who yearned first and foremost to fit in? Were the classic literary masterpieces the meanderings of conventional minds?

Pretend with me that you are the parent of a 14-year-old boy who has taken up with peers who dress in rebellious clothing and hang out on street corners until late in the night—accomplishing nothing more than hanging out. Aside from the cigarette butts decorating the ground and the foul language permeating the air, you sense that the stagnation (with no direction, no goal orientation, and no creativity) can easily lead to misbehavior—a stepping up of the excitement level. Your son is tempted by this band of boys. The idea of being accepted into this group is powerful. He tries to convince you that they are *good* kids. His definition of "good" is that they haven't hurt anything or anybody—yet.

You believe it is unwise for hormonally driven young men to hang out on street corners with no thought of a goal or a potential accomplishment. And you also believe that what now appears to be simple boredom can easily develop into a let's-take-the-thrills-to-the-next-level strategy. You feel certain that after a few more levels, someone is going to get hurt.

I believe most testosterone-driven males are purpose directed—to make that point, to earn their way, to get that girl, to fly in space, to save a life, to invent technology, to build an empire. Boys developing into men push hard to accomplish things in their world. A group of boys who are under-stimulated will seek to become stimulated, and the method they choose may not comport with your family values. Under-stimulation may not be morally wrong, but it can lead to dangerous musings about what can be done next to increase the excitement.

Even though I can predict a power struggle with this boy, at this point I would pick up my resisting child, bring him home, and enroll him in creative physical and intellectual activities with other teenagers—music, theater, writing, reading, ceramics, debate, sports, cars (planes, trains), body building, cooking, karate, or anything else that could teach him new skills, challenge his current abilities, and introduce him to new concepts.

After establishing foundational values and filling my child's life with healthy, stimulating, and fulfilling activities, my next strategy was to emphasize two character traits that parents should be promoting every day—courage and individualism.

Being an individual can't always insulate your children from bad behavior as they assimilate into new groups, fit into a new school, or attempt not to be ostracized or ignored. But instilling individualism (in or out of a group setting) can support your efforts to teach your children to be brave and make good decisions. Tennis shoes are a good example.

We couldn't afford to buy our kids the latest brand of tennis shoes. But our kids had some options: 1) They could accept our budgeted amount and buy an unpopular, unrecognized pair; 2) they could earn the money to pay the difference and get the shoes that fit in; or 3) they could get funky and try something new, as yet untried on the school campus. I was a big fan of Option 3.

I remember the morning one of my sons entered the kitchen dressed and ready for his junior high school day. His feet were protected by an unpopular pair of white tennis shoes, but it was what was hovering above them that caught my eye—two cheerful, bright red socks. He had decided that if he was going to have to deal with a group's arbitrary scale of acceptance, he was going to do it with style. Off he went with his head held high. He was ready to make his statement of individualism.

Did my son get stared at? Yes. Did he get ridiculed? No. What was the result of his bold attire? He was admired—with awe. His daring act paid off big time. Within days, other boys started wearing colorful, playful socks with their tennis shoes. Soon, the type of shoes the male students were wearing took a backseat to the proclamation of the socks—"I am an individual. I extend beyond the crowd." This was a simple and affordable way to assert uniqueness and develop courage.

Going clothes shopping with my daughter was always an experience. She loved belts—eccentric and stylish belts. But the thought of spending what the stores were asking caused me to hyperventilate. Her solution was wrapped in her dad's closet. My daughter sorted through her father's pile of discarded ties. She retired to her room with a handful of vivid and intriguing stripes, dots, flowers, and abstract designs. Afterward, thrift store ties adorned her jeans, hugged her skirts, and controlled her hair. They came in all colors and dimensions. They accented her outfits, they held things up, and they made a clear statement—I am an individual. What is the importance of her proclamation of individuality? That she has the courage to stand alone, that she can choose not to be influenced by the behavior of others, and that she is developing the backbone to make tough decisions, whether she is integrating with a group or on her own.

In his pressure-cooked high school years, my other son joined a club that was not where the popular kids hung out— the academic league, a group that competed scholastically with other schools. Students were bussed to competitor campuses where they were quizzed about history, math, literature, and science. There were time limits. There were bells. There were points and trophies. And there were lots of like-minded kids.

What was my son's reward for being courageous enough to join a group that was most likely held in disdain by the popular kids? He made the best friends of his life. And today, he is still in contact with many of these brave, brotherly souls.

I am not saying that red socks, ties in your hair, or the academic league will lead to good decision making. But I am saying that these are examples of kids developing the courage and individualism necessary to reject everybody's-doing-it bad decisions and to avoid potentially dangerous situations. My children learned to balance the worth of having a group of friends with the value of being an individual. They learned that groups can be good or bad and that they could switch groups or add groups, while remaining individualistic. And they learned that a little creativity and a lot of courage can lead to acceptance as easily as a pair of tennis shoes.

The effect of my children's actions went way beyond acceptance. As I learned much later, it led to admiration. My children were appreciated and respected for extending beyond the conventional mentality of the average teenager. Many of the entries I read in my daughter's senior yearbook stated that her friends wished they had had the courage to do what she did, to be an individual and make her own decisions. Other entries stated they wished they could have been brave enough, like her, *not* to do what everyone else was doing.

Kids create group fashions and trends and engage in certain behaviors to prove that they are individuals—separate and apart from their elders. But the fact that they are all wearing the same shoes, sporting the same hairstyles, dressing in the same clothes, and using the same lingo does not say much about their distinctiveness. I understand that almost every child desires to be part of a group, but I tried to encourage my children to think outside of the box, to extend themselves in a new direction, to be proud of being unique and eccentric, whether they were involved in group dynamics or not.

So my response to the everybody's-doing-it whine was not "You will do it my way or else." My response was, "Do it *your* way."

My children expressed themselves creatively. They developed leadership qualities. They earned respect and admiration. They displayed courage and reaped its rewards. My kids didn't need to smoke or drink to fit in. *They delighted in not fitting in.* They wore scarlet socks on their feet and men's dress ties in their hair. They joined unpopular clubs and organizations. But they didn't hang out in under-stimulating environments. They were much too creative and individualistic for that.

The decisions my kids made to express themselves uniquely and to push past the fear of being left behind earned them the admiration of their peers. As my husband and I partnered with them in our discussions of right and wrong, they became leaders of healthy trends, developers of fresh ideas, and creators of new ways to accomplish things.

Instead of my kids saying, "Mom, everybody's doing it," they were and are proud to say, "Mom, nobody's doing *this.*" The concept of being original and courageous emboldened my children and prepared them to become individuals who demonstrated values and creative interests within a multitude of settings.

 # EXAMPLE

YOUR CHILDREN WILL
FOLLOW YOUR FOOTSTEPS
SOONER THAN FOLLOW
YOUR ADVICE.

In other chapters of this book I wrote about certain child-rearing techniques I used to raise good kids. I covered solid topics like punishment, grades, and chores. But today my adult children tell me that I should not overlook the impact parental role modeling has had on their character.

My husband has been an impressive role model for our children. He has been a walking, breathing example of decency, and the kids have learned so much from him. Because of my husband's upstanding character, my three grown children now acknowledge the importance of marrying a partner who has honor and integrity. I urge all potential parents to think long and hard before they choose the person who will be co-parenting their future children. Marrying my husband was not the luck of the draw. It was a decision I made, and it has affected the moral fiber of my children.

My husband and I did not enter into the parenthood phase

EXAMPLE   43

of our lives with clearly defined parts to play. Our roles in this decades-long family drama evolved. The customary daily discipline of the children was my preference. My husband's choice was to guide by example—to lead an admirable and respectable life. And thank goodness for that. If my husband had taken on the role of disciplinarian, the children would have been able to talk themselves into just about anything. His softhearted nature would not have allowed him to resist teary eyes, pitiful faces, charges of injustice, and bursts of anger. For me, childhood theatrics were no problem. I didn't suffer like my husband did when the kids needed a jolt of reality. In fact, I usually delighted inwardly at their dramatic presentations— before I let the curtain down.

When character issues cropped up, though, my husband's defenses strengthened. At those times he could put his foot down with volcanic force. My husband is tenderhearted, gentle, and kind. And he is principled, honest, and concerned. But you can push him just so far. Like a slender branch, he will bend considerably, but he will not break out of his fortress of standards and values. My children and I admire him and respect him. Unceremoniously he has filled his paternal role as our gentle giant. He has taught our children the significance of being true to a code of ethics.

Now that the kids are grown, I am awed by the contribution my husband has made to their moral fiber. I can see it, feel it, and recognize it. It is evident in the relationships they build, in the everyday decisions they make, and in the paths they choose.

My children's work ethic is a direct result of my husband's solid influence. During every one of their childhood years, they have seen him dedicate himself to his work—professionally and joyfully. In addition, they have seen him continually take on side jobs and extra projects with fervor, in his constant effort to provide for his family and to make our dreams come true. As I watch my children prepare themselves for life's inevitable hurdles, I know that their vision of his dedication and hard work propels them up and over. They can work ceaselessly if need be—without complaint. They present their best work—at all times. They do not stop until the job is done and the end product is one they are proud to sign their names to. They buckle up and bear down. They focus on their tasks and persevere. The work ethic my children have absorbed from their father has provided a foundation upon which a well-built structure can stand.

Honesty and integrity live and thrive under my husband's skin. Like one of those newfangled GPS systems, these two elements of his character are constantly seeking the right path, not the one that is easy. Not the one that will get us by. Not the one that will get us what we want—but the right path. My children have witnessed this firsthand and have integrated the process into their personalities.

My children have seen their father return to the comfort of his home after a tormenting day surrounded by people who were making selfish decisions that he knew were not decent or honorable. They heard the discussions that followed as my husband and I tried to make sense out of some clearly nonsensical situations. I came to the following conclusion: It was no accident that my husband was placed in the middle of a few serious brouhahas. He is my Jiminy Cricket. He takes on the role of the conscience. He has scruples—and the strength to apply them. He is willing to stare potential loss squarely in the face in order to champion a deeper value.

I bless some of those grueling and turbulent times of the past. They provided my children with the opportunity to observe firsthand how to wrestle with another person's lack of integrity and how to turn the course of a painful situation away from potential destruction and toward positive and encouraging results. My children are proud of their father. And the greatest compliment they have given him is to model themselves after his worthy example.

My husband didn't lecture the kids on the importance of contributing to their community. He showed them. His generous expenditures of time and energy have far outweighed the value of any financial contributions we have made. A special antenna

EXAMPLE   45

is implanted in my husband's brain. Although it is invisible to the naked eyes of strangers, it is clearly noticeable to those of us who know and love him. His receiver picks up waves of information about needs in the neighborhood. After he grasps the facts, his citizen's-band-radio brain figures out a way to fill the void. Our children have observed his responses person by person and organization by organization. Today, following his example, our kids delight in the unique contributions they are making. They are proud to share their community activities with us. And we savor the sight of my husband's threads of generosity extending far into the future.

One of the most powerful lessons my husband taught our children is the value of working in a field they are passionate about. My husband truly loves his work! He is excited by it. He is enriched by it. And I don't think he would retire if he had the chance. My children are clearly following in his footsteps.

My oldest son was born to do what he is doing. It has been his singular goal and passion since the age of seven. He was easy. My middle son approached his professional life as if it were a multi-layered onion. He introduced himself to many fields and topics. "That one's nice, but I don't want to dedicate my life to it. And that one's okay, but it doesn't ignite sparks." To him, choosing a profession has been like choosing a life partner. What qualities can I live with, and what qualities can I not? We watched him peel off layer after layer. What was left was a pearl of fascination and attraction—a love affair. Something he could commit himself to—for a lifetime. My daughter had a vague idea, based upon her skills, of the direction she was headed. But it took an inspiring and life-changing summer to motivate her to fine-tune her plans and to dedicate herself to something that made her feel whole.

My husband and I never pressured our children into a particular, high-profile career path. We may have suggested certain disciplines when the topic came up based upon their talents and interests. But they always had the freedom to seek inspiration and steer their course—no matter what the future financial reward would be. My husband taught my children by example that the size of a home and the model of a car do not define one's goodness or happiness. But the passion and joy you have for what you do has a tremendous impact on you, your family, and those you come in contact with.

My husband taught me that loving what you do professionally is a gift you give to your family. His enthusiasm for his work has been luminous. The glow of his infatuation has led each of our children to choose rewarding careers.

And there is so much more. My husband has always had clear goals. And my children have developed clear goals. My husband is committed to his family, his work, and his community. And my children are committed to their relationships, friendships, school, work, and neighborhood. My husband is a protector. He can change into his knight's armor at any moment in order to keep his family members safe. And my children protect their friends and loved ones and help them negotiate life's inevitable twists and turns. My husband uses his time wisely and efficiently. There is no waste here. And my children forge ahead—actively pursuing knowledge and progress. There is no downtime there. My husband is a problem-solver. And my children are following his example.

It is no accident that my children embody so many qualities that I admire. I chose a husband who personified them, and he, by gentle yet sturdy example, has passed them on to my children. By being himself, by setting an example, he has influenced all of our lives. My child-rearing partner watched me dedicate myself to the endless, daily situations that arise in a family dynamic. He was always there to help when I needed him. But much more important was the bar he set for my children. The standards he set for himself were high, and it has been my children's pride and privilege to live up to them. We are so proud of our children's goodness and character. But it is no surprise—these qualities have been passed on to them by design.

FEAR

A GOOD SCARE IS
USUALLY WORTH MORE
THAN GOOD ADVICE.
–Horace

I never wanted my kids to be afraid of me in the sense that they felt terror at the prospect of a beating or panic at the thought of being belittled or humiliated one more time. But I did want my children to "fear" me—in the sense of feeling apprehension, awe, and respect—at certain times. If they felt vulnerable when they were misbehaving, maybe they would stop and think about the possible consequences of their actions. It's hard to describe the worry that I intentionally instilled. But the end result was that my children sensed and concluded that I was in charge and that it was to their advantage to do what I asked—not because they would get a beating if they didn't, but because it was in their best interest to do so.

When kids are toddlers, it is in the family's best interest for them to do what their parents tell them to do—get in the car, get out of the car, eat the food, pick up their food (from the floor, the walls, the furniture), get in the bathtub, get out of the bathtub. The family must move on—to the next stop, the next event, the next meal, the next night's sleep. Once my small children understood the family hierarchy and realized that their parents were the alpha members, they started cooperating for reasons of their own—family harmony, empathy for others, comprehension of the situation, and reduced tension in their lives. If my children respected my authority when they were young, I could use that influence to direct their behavior and ease them into the next growth stage.

Children can try your patience. And yes, there are times when parents lose control. Occasionally, we give a swat on the behind to protect our kids from imminent danger or because we are exasperated and have run out of other things to try. But generally speaking, on run-of-the mill days, I learned that there were some easy techniques I could implement to get the result I was looking for: kids who were motivated to cease a dangerous or annoying behavior, and a family pecking order in which I was clearly the person in charge. In order for my children to learn how to behave in a complex society filled with many people, things, and choices, I needed them to fear (awe, respect) me and to learn that I had the final word.

When I was in my 20s and my kids were small, asserting power was not easy for me. But as a young parent, I knew that if I wanted my children to stop or change a testing behavior, I had to act like an authority figure. I struggled through "power boot camp" and eventually promoted myself from private to general. After that, my foot-soldier children stepped right into line.

The first technique I utilized to create trepidation (awe, respect) in an unruly child was eye contact. Eye contact helped me direct my children's behavior simply, easily, and effectively. When I say "eye contact," I mean in-your-face eye contact. This was often hard to do with a straight face. The disruptive behavior my children were engaged in was usually so comical or creative that I had to work hard to keep myself from revealing my amusement. But I pulled myself together and struggled to display my "angry face." I stooped down to their level and positioned my hardened features inches from their faces. When my children saw "that look," they stopped in their tracks. The "uh-oh" expression on their faces was obvious. I could sense the gears turning as they began to contemplate what they had done and how their lives would be affected by it. Often "the look" was the only tool I needed to turn an unruly child around.

But life wasn't always that simple. As my children became more sophisticated, I developed a multi-pronged approach. When "the look" alone did not do the trick, I added another step—the dreaded "pointer finger." If you were to ask my grown children today what childhood memory left them trembling in terror, they would tell you it was "Mom's pointer finger." And they would also tell you that they haven't yet figured out exactly why it worked or what the threat was. But they definitely recall that it was menacing.

I used my pointer finger as a tool to enforce "the look." And it proved to be a handy instrument. I used my finger to make physical contact with my child. I placed my finger—sometimes gently and sometimes with some pressure—on one of their soft, chubby cheeks. As I saw the foreboding grow in their eyes, I fought the impulse to comfort them. I kept the pressure of my pointer finger constant while I continued to impart "the look."

If "the look" and the "finger" didn't accomplish the goal of stopping or changing a disagreeable or dangerous behavior, I stepped up a notch to "the voice." During these more serious episodes, my voice rolled out of my mouth in a low, deep pitch—almost a growl. My voice didn't have to be loud. Sometimes (in public places) it was only a whisper. But the sound of it could induce a cold sweat—especially when combined with "the look" and "the finger." When utilizing "the voice," I spoke slowly and deliberately, never taking my eyes off of my child's eyes and never releasing my physical contact point, my finger. The result—boy, did they listen to what I had to say. They understood that I meant business. When my children sensed "the voice" heading their way, they decided that it was in their best interest to stop the offending behavior—immediately.

When my daughter read the rough draft of this chapter, she

said, "Mom, don't forget counting to three." I had forgotten, but she had not. Apparently, counting to three had made an impression on her. "One-two-three" was a tool I used to guide my children's behavior, and it was used for situations like loud or unruly behavior at someone else's house, screaming in the playground when it was time to leave, or refusing to get dressed in the morning. "One" meant, "It's time to think about stopping whatever you are doing—or starting whatever you are supposed to start." "Two" meant, "Mom is getting serious." And "three" meant, "If you continue for one more second, you are going to suffer an immediate consequence."

My children never found out if there was a Number 4 because they never even made it to Number 3. Offending behaviors always stopped after I said "Twooooooooo" very slowly with my pitch going up at the end. To be honest, I never even knew what my next step would be if I were forced to say "three." It's fortunate for me that my first two attempts were as easy as one-two-three.

As a young parent, I was never certain that my techniques were going to work. I was a fly-by-the-seat-of-my-pants kind of mom. I let my intuition shape my simple steps to good behavior. If one method didn't work, I tried something else that I thought would create the fear (awe, respect) and the pecking order that was necessary for us to live together in a harmonious household. The routine I developed established me as the authority figure. It caused no physical pain or harm to my children. It did not destroy their spirits. It did not diminish their self-respect. It was a clear statement that "Mom is in charge here." The only threat my children felt was a perceived threat—a threat that they imagined: "What would happen if Mom says 'three'?"

One convenient element of my four-pronged parenting program (face, finger, voice, and counting) is that I carried the tools with me wherever I went. At home, I could voice my concern with a little more volume. But in public, I could get the same results without ever speaking above a whisper. My finger was always there, ready for contact. And my eyes were always eager to stare into my children's faces.

The four-pronged program was activated when my children were displaying annoying behaviors or they needed to learn a lesson. If danger was imminent, like stepping off a curb when a car was approaching, I certainly did not take the time to count to three. I grabbed the clueless kid and moved him to safety as quickly as possible. Once that child was safe and sound, we could have a serious conversation about what just happened. If a character issue, like dishonesty or disrespect, was exposed, I assigned a more immediate and serious consequence—again to be followed by a sober discussion. But for the average, everyday little things, my "fear" system worked beautifully.

When I introduced fear (awe, respect) into my relationship with my children, they learned some important things: that they could *not* do whatever they wanted whenever they wanted to; that they were *not* the center of the universe but part of an intricate web of interconnecting relationships; and that other people have needs too—for quiet, order, and tranquility. If they hesitated to learn the lesson I was attempting to teach them, they knew there would be further consequences. Lucky for me, it was rarely necessary for us to go that far.

A little bit of friendly fear can help parents raise children who acknowledge the needs of the people around them. Nobody likes to be around a selfish adult. Parents can help to encourage cooperation and avoid egocentricity by using some simple tools: a focused look, a pointer finger, a surly voice, and the number three.

 FOOD

Children who are picky eaters complicate the lives of their families. Parents of these children burden themselves when they prepare one meal for the majority (trout almandine with sautéed green beans and saffron rice) and another meal for the minority (macaroni and cheese). They encumber waiters with a complicated mix of special orders—"A cheeseburger without the meat, please." They inconvenience hosts at social events—"Can my son have his hot dog wrapped in a slice of white bread instead of a bun, please?"

I love food. My children love food. My husband merely likes food. He could work right through lunch and never skip a beat. To me, that would be akin to torture. But whether we love food or like food, each person in my family eats *all* kinds of food. Mexican food tops the list, as it does for any decent Southern Californian. We live for Anita's Quesadilla Ole and Poncho's Surprise. But we also look forward to Chicken Saag at our favorite Indian restaurant, Hot Basil Chicken at our preferred Thai cafe, and Vegetable Tempura at our special Japanese bistro. We enjoy Spanish food and Sri Lankan food, and on and on and on. We are on a global, ethnic eating plane.

In contrast, I have heard many negative culinary comments from our children's friends: "What is *this*?" This particular comment is usually accompanied by a scrunched face and a look of disgust. Or "I don't eat anything with green in it (or yellow or red)." Or "I don't like the texture of this. It's too squishy." Then there is the popular, "Yuck," which usually is uttered while the appalled child-guest is poking the entrée I so lovingly prepared with his or her fork. I have seen kids turn down homemade New Orleans squash soup, witnessed the revulsion on their faces when I served Mediterranean salmon smothered in sautéed olives and onions, and heard them admit to me that they only eat chicken nuggets, French fries, and pizza.

Keeping food in balance with the other parts of our lives is important. Whatever parents choose to make an issue out of seems to be what their children decide to rebel against, so it is important that parents choose their battles wisely. With that idea in mind, I didn't want to force food behaviors on my children. I realized that making food an issue could contribute to future mutinous acts of overeating, under-eating, or obsession. So food wasn't an issue in our home. Food was beloved. There was a natural intake and joy that accompanied it. "Sure, you can have some chips. Just put some in a bowl. Don't eat out of the bag, please." "If you are too full to finish your dinner, it's okay to stop eating." "Yes, you can have a cookie. Just eat it after dinner, please." "You don't want to eat the peas? Okay. Just try one. If you don't want any more after that, no problem."

Cooking was one tool I used to create and maintain food balance in our home. Enticing aromas! Aaaah! Spices do delight the senses, so instead of serving foods with preservatives, dyes, and fillers, I flavored my foods with cumin, cardamom, garam masala, and zatar. By venturing out beyond hot dogs and hamburgers, I enriched my children's lives and palates. To this day, I most enjoy cooking things I have never attempted before: Indian dishes, Mediterranean dishes, Cajun dishes, and more. And the kids like that, too. But they still have their family favorites. They still love Mom's enchiladas, tacos, chili, and soups. And I am pleased to honor their requests.

How do parents tempt a child's palate to appreciate a diversity of foods? How do parents teach their children to welcome food as the sensory delight it is: a mix of textures, aromas, colors, flavors, and sounds (like the crackling of fajitas on a hot, cast iron skillet)? Each food item bursts with a unique blend of nutritional ingredients: beta carotene, antioxidants, Omega 3s, vitamins, minerals, protein, and carbohydrates. How can we as parents ensure that our children are digesting the variety of elements they need to maintain mental and physical health? Here are some stories that may help answer those questions.

When my oldest son was big enough to sit in a high chair, we received permission from his pediatrician to start him on certain approved solid foods. We were very careful to not stray from the doctor's list. When he said "rice cereal," we stuck to packaged rice cereal. When he said "fruit," we chose pallid jars of watery produce. My son thought the rice cereal, which had the texture of wet cement, and the smooshed fruit, which had the look of slimy goop, were okay, but they certainly didn't excite his baby palate.

One day, when my husband and I went out for a short while, we left the baby with a sitter. On the stove was a big pot of simmering, spicy lentil soup. When we returned, the sitter was spoon-feeding the baby volumes of this soup—onions, garlic, carrots, celery, seasonings, and all. And what do you know? He absolutely loved it, and with no negative digestive repercussions. Now, I am certainly not suggesting that you disobey your doctor's orders and feed your babies lentil soup. But I am saying that kids appreciate home-cooked food that is lovingly prepared by their parents.

After that episode, I bought a portable baby food grinder. This grinder turned out to be my closest companion for many,

many years. I never again opened a jar of tasteless squished peaches again. I started grinding fresh fruit, replete with its full spectrum of vitamins and minerals. I no longer added water to dehydrated cereals. I now cooked my own healthy cereals and ran them through the grinder. Soon, my young children were eating what we had for breakfast, what we had for lunch, and what we had for dinner. The spices I used in my international dishes whetted their appetites to try more. We didn't go anywhere without that grinder. It traveled with us to restaurants, friends' houses, amusement parks, and more.

I am a mom who cooked when my children were small and who still cooks now that they are out of the house (because I enjoy it as a creative endeavor). I am not saying that we never went out for pizza, because we certainly did. But, pretty much, our routine was that on Monday through Friday we enjoyed home cooking, and on weekends we enjoyed some restaurant fare. By taking the time to plan for and cook at home, I was able to regulate the foods my children were ingesting. I could introduce a diversity of spices and flavors, and control the nutritional content of their diets. It took a little organizing, but it was very doable.

Usually, I cooked in the late afternoon or early evening. But if the day's schedule didn't allow for that, I chopped and diced in the morning and merely threw everything together in the afternoon. If I knew I had a busy week coming up, I cooked one or two entrees on the weekend and then stored them for future use. And I saved a lot of time by limiting my trips to the grocery store to one trip per week—no matter what. If we ran out of something, we ran out of it. I got very creative at assigning substitutes. This once-a-week-grocery philosophy saved me precious time and lots of effort. All I had to do was plan my meals ahead of time: Monday might have been enchiladas with guacamole, salad, and Spanish rice; Tuesday might have been roast Cajun chicken with garlic mashed potatoes, salad, and green beans. And so on. I created my list. I shopped for the week. Then I put on my magic New Orleans apron and pushed the button on my CD player. Voila! I was transformed into a celebrity chef.

What did I do if one of my children didn't want to try something new, something that looked a little different? We had a rule: Take one bite. If you don't like what you taste, you can pass on that item and enjoy the rest of your meal. But passes were not allowed unless there was a try. I remember my children's cautious looks as they gingerly placed a teaspoon of spinach soufflé or broccoli quiche into their barely open mouths. Usually they liked what they tasted. But if they didn't, I never forced them to eat something they didn't like. Why? Because I am still nursing memories from my early childhood when I was forced to sit at the table until my soggy canned peas were gone. I tried to hide them under my plate. I tried to drop them onto my napkin. I tried to feed them to the dog. But when those techniques didn't work, I sat there, usually crying and ready to heave, until my plate was empty. My parents thought they were doing what was best for me, forcing warm green pebbles of nutrition down my throat. But I wanted to be respected for my likes and dislikes, especially when I was opening my mind and mouth to new experiences.

When my children were older and decided that they didn't like a meal I had prepared, I said, "Fine. You can make your own dinner. Just make sure it has nutritional value." I *never, ever* got up from the table to make a second dinner for a fussy eater. I simply continued enjoying my meal and told them to go ahead and make their own. Well, they quickly tired of the culinary effort. In a very short while, they were back at the table eating with the rest of the family.

We had sweet snacks and dessert foods in our home all the time—ice cream, cookies, and some candy here and there— but these items existed so naturally in our surroundings that they never became an obsession. They were simply there—on the counter and in the cupboard 24 hours a day. I credit the attitude of peaceful coexistence with junk food with protecting my children from fixating on empty calories. They didn't *need* to gorge on sugar because they knew that any time they had a craving, it was there. I have seen children whose parents would not allow them to take one bite of a cookie or one lick of a lollipop. When those kids got to my house, they went absolutely berserk. If I offered them a cookie, they wanted the whole box. If I offered them a sucker, they wanted the whole bag. They didn't want to limit themselves because they didn't know when the next opportunity would arise. (Of course, I never offered a sweet snack to a child whose parents told me they had sugar restrictions.)

As I was teaching food lessons to my children, they were busy teaching me as well. My oldest son's 9th birthday party is a good example. My husband and I planned the festivities at a wonderful restaurant that offered a full ice cream bar for dessert, every flavor and topping you could imagine. My son enjoyed his hearty buffet meal—he ate it all. When he was done, I took his hand in mine and said, "It's time to go to the ice cream bar!" His answer floored me. It was short. It was simple. It was complete. He responded, "I am full." My frenzied response was this: "What has that got to do with anything? What does feeling full have to do with eating ice cream?"

I couldn't comprehend at that time what my son was telling me. He had a healthy relationship with food. So when his tummy told him that the door was closed, he listened. I am ashamed to admit how hard I tried to get him to eat some ice cream that day, but I soon realized that there was no way he was going to partake. Instead, he watched, played, and laughed as the other partygoers enjoyed their desserts. He left that restaurant without having tasted one bite of birthday ice cream. I am still awed by that. And to this day I try to follow his lead—I try to stop eating when I am full.

Today, my kids go to all kinds of restaurants and try all kinds of foods, just as they always have. Food is easy for them. They have no struggles with too much, too little, too spicy, too bland, too weird, or too plain. But that was part of my overall plan. A modest baby food grinder, a few aromatic spices, some good home cooking, and a little balance have created the healthy relationship my kids share with food.

FREEDOM AND TRUST

THE BASIC TEST OF
FREEDOM IS PERHAPS LESS
IN WHAT WE ARE FREE TO
DO THAN IN WHAT WE
ARE FREE NOT TO DO.
—ERIC HOFFER.

". . . with liberty and justice for all." When my children were young, I thought long and hard about the amount of freedom I was going to bestow upon them. Would it be too much or too little? I continued to mull over the complexities of this issue throughout their high school years and their college initiations. The philosophy I experimented with and communicated to my offspring was this: Right now you have a certain amount of freedom (whatever I felt was appropriate for their age at the time), and you have our trust. We will maintain this arrangement—*unless. . . .*

As soon as my children were old enough to learn right from wrong, we gave them the gift of age-appropriate freedom and trust. I liken this idea to starting off the school year with a report card chock-full of A's. The only way they could have lost their freedom or our trust was through their deeds (commission or omission).

By adopting this viewpoint, I learned something significant:

that *earning our trust was even more important to my children than their freedom*. Today my kids tell me that the most devastating thing that could have happened to them when they were growing up was to lose the trust of their parents. They had more opportunities to make their own decisions and to express their independence than most of their friends, and they were grateful. But they knew that the root of that freedom was our confidence in them to do the right thing.

Let's take curfews, for example. I know this is going to sound bizarre to many of you readers, but my teenagers had no curfews. What they had instead was an opportunity to demonstrate to us that 1) they were responsible, 2) they could make healthy choices, 3) they could handle a variety of situations maturely, and 4) they were respectful of our thoughts, feelings, and desires.

How did I come to adopt what might seem to you to be illogical logic—giving freedom to teenagers? The answer can be found in my childhood. I was a good and well-behaved kid. Even so, my parents assaulted me with "unfair" rules and regulations—for my own protection. I remember being invited out on a Saturday night and enjoying the company of peers (something that is very important to the developing identity of an adolescent). I also recall being forced to tear myself away from a rewarding social connection because of an arbitrary deadline. Why was 10:58 P.M. okay but 11:03 P.M. was not? I remember often thinking, "I will *never* do that to my children." When I became a parent, I stuck to my teenage guns.

When I was a teenager, I thought that the people most important to me, my parents, did not seem to trust my judgment. I felt overprotected. My spirit of independence was being pushed deep into a dark crevice, hopefully to resurface one day. I lost confidence in my ability to handle life and make decisions on my own. I felt frustration at not being able to live in the moment. Yes, I was loved. Yes, I was protected. But something in me longed for freedom and my parents' trust.

As a parent, I reversed the rules that were forced on me as

a minor. I dropped the idea of a curfew. I added the idea that my children's behavior today would define their tomorrow. My husband and I gave our kids freedom—to make wise decisions and continue as is *or* to act irresponsibly and change their current, unencumbered course drastically. In return, they owed us respect—to know where they were going, who they were going with, what activity they were going to be engaged in, and about what time they planned to be home. If they were going to return later than the stated time, they owed us a phone call so that we could sleep peacefully, secure in the knowledge that they were safe.

I took a risk with this no-curfew philosophy, and I learned something valuable. The vast majority of times, my kids were home *much* earlier than we had expected. They had no rebellion to express—because there was nothing to rebel against. They didn't need to demonstrate their independence—because it was understood. So when the evening began to lose its luster, they preferred to unlock the door to their welcoming home, enter its comfortable surroundings, and enjoy the knowledge that tomorrow they would relish more freedom, decision making, and trust—because they had *earned* it.

Sometimes I wondered if I was doing the right thing. After all, my teenage children possibly could have been exposed to parties I would rather they not attend, to alcohol, or to drugs. But my children knew that those were exactly the types of activities that would cause them to lose their freedom. I often queried my children about why they had returned early the night before. Almost always it was because their peers had been drinking (or worse), and they did not want to be exposed to the people or the behaviors.

One day I asked one of my sons how the beach party was the night before. I was surprised by his answer: "I spent the entire evening pulling drunks out of a fire pit. It was awful." The result: One early night home! My daughter once shared with me, "People who are high have no idea how ridiculous they look and act and how boring they can be. When kids

act like that, I want to get as far away from them as possible."
Another early night home! When my other son was a college
freshman, he expressed his distaste for the party scene. He was
disappointed by the behaviors of his peers. They went out of
control in an effort to assert their independence and freedom.
Many early nights home!

I never had to deal with drunk, drugged, or wild children.
My kids each found a circle of friends who, like them, did not feel
the need to rebel—friends who could share time, conversation,
music, and fun—*creatively*. With drug- and alcohol-free minds,
my children enjoyed imaginative outlets and intellectual
stimulation.

For example, one day, one of my sons wanted to spoof the
students who drove around in cars that blasted pulsating, ear-
piercing music. He and his friends—all music lovers—got in an
old, cheap, faded sedan, and blasted polka tunes as they drove
around the high school campus. Another day my daughter had
a group of friends huddled in her bedroom. When I walked
down to see how they were doing, I found them engrossed in a
heated debate on stem cell research and cloning. My other son
performed in a group that had to provide its own props. Their
act required a cow. So they spent days building a handsome,
brown-eyed, papier-mâché cow. My children found these types
of activities a lot more fulfilling than spending time in dark,
smoky rooms filled with stupefied, unmotivated peers.

There are so many healthy ways for our kids to be original,
creative, and joyful. My children appreciated their freedom, and
they understood the importance of *earning* our trust. They were
determined to keep our trust and, thus, maintain their level of
liberty. They chose friends and activities that supported their
healthy lifestyles. And they avoided those things that could
prove to be detrimental.

When I was a young adult, I lost my sense of independence
for a while. But thanks to a patient, loving, and supportive
husband, I was able to unearth it and win it back—as an adult.
But my children have been spared that challenge. They learned

to make wise decisions at an early age. They earned the trust of their parents and learned to trust themselves. They became very resourceful and were in full command of their activities. In addition, they were sensitive to our needs.

Today, my children say, "We never wanted to mess with a good thing." As a result, they created many other good things: harmony in the household; solid relationships with friends; the ability to express themselves creatively, joyfully, and healthfully; behavior that was responsible and thought-through; the capacity to weigh outcomes; an appreciation of liberty; and the warmth of their parents' trust.

Building character is about making choices. If I had removed my children's autonomy—if I had grounded them for a month for coming home five minutes late (a situation I have actually witnessed in other families)—I would have eliminated their options and robbed them of the opportunity to prove themselves. Our home environment invited our children to make many decisions on their own. And over and over again, they chose well—they chose freedom and trust.

FRIENDS

ONE'S FRIENDS ARE THAT
PART OF THE HUMAN RACE
WITH WHICH ONE CAN BE
HUMAN.
—Santayana

Don't underestimate the power peer relationships have over your children. All of your value-instilling techniques can come to naught if your children choose to hang out with cohorts who do not live by your family's standards. The desire children have to fit in is compelling and intense. And the things they do in the name of acceptance can cause parents to shake their heads and wonder, "What were you thinking?"

As a new parent trying to formulate my thoughts on childhood friendships, I struggled with two competing ideas. Number one, I wanted to ensure that my kids were surrounded by peers who came from families who had values similar to ours. Number two, I wanted to give my children license to choose friends who represented a diversity of ideas and thoughts.

My solution to these contradictory concepts was to give my children freedom to make their own friends—within boundaries. As my kids began to build friendships, I was anxiously hoping they would make choices that would keep me at arm's length and prevent me from stepping in and setting boundaries. This freedom-within-boundaries viewpoint touched many aspects of our family life.

First, there was school. I knew that my children's neighborhood playmates and schoolyard friends would be picked from the "school pool." When the backpack, lunch-pail years arrived, our family was living in a lovely community that housed a large transient population. As a result, the school's academic scores were low, and student swaggering and intimidation were high. My husband and I wanted one thing socially and academically for our children, but we had another. What was our solution? We moved. It wasn't easy to pack up a family of five. Boxes overflowed and muscles bulged as we lifted bundles into cars, out of cars, and into a new place. We moved to a neighboring community where families were committed to settling down and staying put. Parents were involved in local activities and visible in the schools. Academics were high. Student swaggering and intimidation were low. I am sure there was trouble to be had on the playground, but it was going to be a little bit harder for my kids to find.

I understand that many families cannot simply pick up and move, but for us, it was a good solution with beneficial results. Once they were enrolled in their new schools, our kids had a different type of challenge—being the new kid on the block. And they were nervous about it. But I trusted that my children were likable enough to overcome the new-kid hurdle, and I was right.

Next, it was important to ensure that my children were involved in school activities and youth groups. Why? Because that is how children make friends—playing sports *together*, creating art *together*, making music *together*, acting in theater *together*, writing stories *together*, collecting rocks and geodes *together*. Finding common ground meant finding friends— companions my kids could talk to and relate to about things they enjoyed doing *together*. My children didn't have to search desperately for a miscellaneous pal. Their friends were at their side, enjoying what they enjoyed. The groups my children were engaged in were small and easy to negotiate. And the children my kids were spending time with came from families who also encouraged physical activity, creativity, and engaged minds.

After my children had made some friends, it was important to open up my home to them. A mess of toys littered the floor, high-pitched noises permeated the air, and dirty dishes decorated the kitchen countertop. But the rewards were huge. By inviting my children's peers into our house on family day trips (to movie theaters, the beach, and the zoo) and on family vacations (to campgrounds, hiking sites, and amusement parks), I was signaling to my children that I approved of their choices and that I, too, enjoyed the company of their playmates.

In the comfortable surroundings of our home I observed how my children interacted with others. I guided them, when necessary, on sharing their space, their things, and their time. While they were eating peanut butter on celery sticks in the kitchen, I joked and chatted with the group and got a sense of who these playmates were. I explained personality quirks to my children. I encouraged a sense of tolerance as I described how some traits are endearing and others are challenging. I discussed how best to deal with tricky social situations as they came up. Inviting my children's playmates into my home gave me a window through which I glimpsed and guided my children's social development and through which I examined the character of the kids my children chose to spend time with.

I learned quickly not to make direct negative comments about their friends to my children. They considered their relationships with their friends to be personal. One unenthusiastic remark from me caused my kids to shrink away from further discussion. Why? They considered their friends to be an extension of themselves. If I didn't like a friend that they felt connected to, they reacted as if I didn't like the part of them that bonded to this person and that I didn't trust their ability to choose well.

I discovered a way to communicate my observations without my children feeling judged and without closing the door between us. I asked a lot of questions. "That was fun at the pizza parlor. What did you think about Jonathan running wildly and bumping into that poor lady who sat silently sipping her Coke?" Because I wasn't accusing his friend, my child felt free to respond uninhibitedly. He may have replied, "I didn't like it when Jonathan was so wild. I felt bad for the lady who got Coke on her shirt." His response opened the door for me to add my lesson, "Yes. It's nicer for *everyone* in the restaurant when kids walk instead of run, isn't it?"

As the years went by, the friendship process offered challenges to me and my children. For example, what if they brought someone home whom I suspected had a weak character or a rebellious heart? Should I prohibit my child from spending time with this friend? Before I ever initiated a tough, separation stance, I decided to wait and see what my children would do with the challenge. Would they figure it out themselves? With years of friendship training behind them, my children did figure it out, independently of me, and usually very quickly. There was only one instance in which I was forced to prohibit a child from visiting our home. When I approached my son to tell him so, he knew it and wanted it before I ever uttered a word.

And what about the high school friend who entered my home wearing clothing that would make the average person stare and hair that would glorify the local mosh pit? Again, I decided to be consistent. I waited to see what my child decided to do. And what did I discover? Below the caricature was a sweet, kind-hearted, lovable, creative, and intellectually stimulating child. This time, *the lesson was mine*. I learned not to judge a book by its cover. I learned to delve into the storyline and appreciate its charm.

It was important to my children that I understood their social styles and then *let them be*. I had one child who was socially cautious. He preferred to watch and absorb the behavior of others before he proceeded to make initial contact. If he had to spend a little time alone as he conducted his research, he was comfortable with that. The playground was his laboratory. His task was to observe, reach a conclusion, make a move, and get results—when he was ready and confident to do so. This child preferred a smaller group of long-lasting, close-knit friends. Today, he still enjoys a relationship with most of these school buddies.

My second son has always been surrounded by lots of friends, and has always had a leadership role. At one point, when we were switching him from one school environment to another, a group of families did the same thing at the same time because their kids wanted to be wherever he was. He now has friendships with people who are spread all over the world. Old friends, new friends. Gold friends, silver friends. They are different ages and have different interests. They enrich his life in a multitude of ways.

My daughter wanted *these* friends, but ended up with *other* friends. She wanted to be part of *this* group, but ended up being part of *another* group. Her friendships were fluid, never on a straight course. She has carried a few friends with her from childhood, but she prefers trying new things and making new friends. Her relationships are often ebbing and flowing. What looked on the surface to be bright and inviting one day, proved to be disappointing and frustrating the next. She delves deeply, and she prefers not to "waste" her time on someone who she feels will disappoint her. She is in no way antisocial; she merely has learned that spending quiet time (which can include blasting music, if that makes any sense) alone often can be more satisfying than being disillusioned by another purported friend.

When my daughter read this chapter, she surprised me by saying, "You should include how you actually *talked* to our friends." She said that it was rare to find that quality in other parents, especially to the extent her dad and I did it. She added, "If parents take the time to learn about the friends, they can judge if they are good people and learn a lot about their own child as a result."

Why was I astonished when she said this? Because every time her dad or I started up a conversation with one of her teenage friends, she was standing on the sidelines rolling her eyes, as if we were the biggest embarrassments in the universe. In her senior year of high school, though, she had an epiphany. Her friends liked us and enjoyed talking to us *because* we expressed so much interest in them. No need to be embarrassed after all. In fact, she ended up being proud. We all had lessons to learn in the friendship department.

I was lucky with the friend thing. Almost always, my children gravitated to terrific kids. If I felt uneasy with a particular child, it wasn't long before my kids came to the same conclusion. What did we do to contribute to their decision making? We enrolled them in the right school. We opened our home to our children's friends, and we got to know them. We encouraged our kids to participate in active and creative pursuits. We honored each child's unique friendship style. We were careful about judging but insistent on getting our messages across in other ways. We talked to our children's friends.

I feel fortunate that I never had to enforce my will regarding my children's friends. I suspect that a family conflict over a childhood friendship could be intense and devastating. My middle child told me about some studies that suggest that peers have a greater influence on our developing personalities than parents do. That may be hard to hear, but it means that parents have to take this subject seriously. While some children are naturally attracted to friends who like "good, clean fun," others learn their lessons by making mistakes. The friendship lessons we learn and the challenges we overcome enhance our lives forever.

GRADES

"Do you pay for grades?" This is a question parents often ask other parents. Every parent is trying hard to discover the magic solution to the not-so-straight-A dilemma. How do parents encourage their kids to be responsible and perform their best at school *for themselves and for a lifetime*, versus doing it for an arbitrary reward in a random instance?

While our kids are on the playground kicking a soccer ball or enjoying a peanut butter and jelly sandwich with friends, their parents are concentrating on getting them into college and setting them up in a lifetime career. No wonder grades are an area of potential conflict. Parents and children are not even on the same planet. The kids are living for the present, and the parents are living for the future. And sometimes the parents are muddying the water with their own pasts as well.

I was paid for grades as a child (a dollar for A's and 50 cents for B's), but I did not continue the tradition. By the time my kids were in elementary school, I felt that it was their *obligation and duty* to earn good grades. To me, getting decent grades was not something to be viewed as extraordinary or beyond the scope of their everyday responsibilities. School was their present life's work. And the grades they achieved *were* the reward—the reward they merited based on the energy they put forth. I felt it was important that my children performed their best in school and that they did it *for themselves*—not for an outside incentive. The future benefits that resulted from their dedication to schoolwork would come in the form of doors opening and opportunities unfolding. My children's access to the work world would be commensurate with the level of commitment and effort they exerted in school.

We did celebrate grades though. When report cards came out and the kids performed well (not straight A's, but well enough), we went out—to dinner, that is. On a rotating basis, the kids chose the restaurant. We then spent (usually over chips and salsa) a lively evening discussing their classes, their teachers, and their grades. The children basked in the joy of our interest in their studies and our pride in their performance. These dinners were not rewards. They happened regardless of the grades printed on the report cards. Instead, the dinners celebrated milestones—another semester passed, another year completed. A's, B's, and C's were not an issue in our family. Anything lower would have been viewed as a signal to me that my husband or I needed to spend more time explaining a confusing concept, or that a tutor might be worth considering.

My kids were always encouraged to do their best. After all, they couldn't do any better than that. And if their best was a B or a C, then we cheered that B or that C. We honored course content, the relationships they established with teachers, and the energy and concentration they applied.

When my children came home from school, they had a very short winding-down snack time. Then they were back to the books. The quicker they finished their homework, the more time they had to play. This routine—obligations first and play later—prevented many late and exhausting nights and established priorities, the first of which was my kids' responsibility to get their work done. I felt that conscientious behavior would take my children far, irrespective of what their individual grades turned out to be.

My middle son says that, to this day, he completes his obligations quickly. He doesn't like the feeling in the pit of his stomach when important tasks pile up. So he still works first and plays later. When he dedicates himself to the many activities that balance his life—like friends, music, and mountain unicycling— he is able to do so with gusto. Because of his responsibility habit, the stomach tension is gone, replaced by the comforting knowledge that his free time truly is free.

I have always taught my children that *a little bit of stress* is nothing to be afraid of. In fact, it can be a great motivator. It can spur us to fulfill our obligations, accomplish great things, and enjoy our activities with healthy abandon. But when irresponsible behavior piles things too high, a debilitating stress level can result. This anxiety can keep us from enjoying any aspects of our busy lives. Staying on top of their obligations has enabled my children to control their angst and to function continuously at a high level of performance—at work and at play.

The two most vital components of my children's school life were balance (academics *plus* physical activity *plus* community involvement *plus* artistic endeavors *plus* social activities and friendships) and passion. There is so much more to learn at school than grades represent. How about the joy of developing new skills through sports and the arts? How about the excitement of rushing from your vigorous water polo meet to your demanding academic competition? Or from your peer counseling session with a troubled teen to your award-winning show choir performance? Or from your soaring pole vaulting meet to your lead in *The Importance of Being Ernest*? How about the exhileration of meeting friends who have the same vitality, enthusiasm, and interests you do? How about the thrill of falling into bed at night feeling satisfied with your day and your life?

I was never concerned whether my children got into Stanford or Yale. Rather, I was dedicated to the notion that my children would attend the college they *deserved* to attend. If it happened to be Stanford, I had no problem with that. But if it happened to be much less prestigious, that was fine with me too. In fact, if my kids had decided that the career they were interested in was achieved through vocational education in a field like welding or through certificate training in a field like hotel management, I would have slept equally well at night.

When my children entered college they were amazed and excited by the scope of the course offerings. Their only frustration was that they didn't have enough time to take every class in the catalog. (And they still feel that way.) One of my children approached this delightful dilemma scientifically. As a freshman, he decided to take a course in every general category that interested him. He then decided whether he was attracted enough to delve into that category further. If not, he went on to the next area of study. After eliminating several departments, he proceeded to fine-tune his choices within accepted subjects of interest. Soon, he was able to narrow his search to topics that truly excited and fascinated him. Now *these* he could spend a lifetime pursuing.

I never had a stake in my kids' future careers. I never stressed out about them being doctors or lawyers or professors. What was important to me was that they discovered interests that they were passionate about and that they had the gumption to follow through with them. In our home, school was a giant research laboratory. We experimented with this (theater, chorus, musical instruments) and we experimented with that (swim team, water polo, pole vaulting, dance). We tested the waters through clubs, civic organizations, academic competitions, and peer counseling. Grades were part of my children's lives, a very important part. But they were never the only part or the most significant part.

It was not important to me whether my children's choices eventually earned them $40,000 a year or $400,000 a year. A person earning a modest salary could be happier living in a log cabin encircled by a verdant forest than a person earning an enviable salary living in a mansion surrounded by celebrities. As long as they learned to live within their means and to maintain their enthusiasm and their balance, I could foresee great things.

So I didn't pay for grades, and I didn't stress over them either. Instead, I guided my children through the school maze by inspiring them to try many different activities; experiment with many different tools; and expand their skills, talents, and knowledge base on a regular basis. Some of this testing led to beloved, lifelong hobbies: mountain unicycling, musical instruments (guitar, piano, banjo, clarinet, gamelan, voice), hiking and backpacking, and photography. Other research led to career choices that will bring a lifetime of joy and fulfillment to my children. People who enjoy what they do every day do not come home depleted. They come home energized and ready to share—with their spouses, their children, and their communities.

My children now have the lives they *earned and deserve*, and they are at peace with them. Not because I paid them for grades, but because they were inspired to discover what stimulated them and to follow that course *for themselves*. In lieu of an expectation of straight A's, my husband and I expected them to do their best and motivated them to work to their fullest potential. We did that by showing *interest* in and *excitement* for what they learned at school. We asked them questions that encouraged dialogue about particular topics. We exposed them to information about a variety of career paths—some that were well known and others that were hidden from view. We taught them the importance of having passion for what you do every day. We set ourselves up to be examples of dependable adults who fulfill obligations.

It was my children's responsibility to earn what they now have, and it is their privilege to enjoy it. They have chosen their paths. They have become accomplished and capable. Their balanced lives are a tribute to their journey. Now, my job is easy.

I get to sit back, relax, and take pleasure in the many activities and contributions they continually share with me.

HUMILIATION

An adorable toddler taught me that children—little children—can and do suffer humiliation. I have a clear memory of the day I learned that lesson. My oldest child was just 14 months old, and his chubby little legs were in training. They were preparing him for the running, jumping, and sliding days that were fast approaching. As I watched, he pulled his bulk upward and forced one wobbly leg to lift its mass and land unsteadily in front of the other. The movement was tentative, but he was tenacious. The drive to move forward consumed him.

This teetering toddler was the first child, the first grandchild, the first nephew, the first grand experience in our family. And we—parents, grandparents, aunts, uncles, and friends—delighted in his every move. He laughed and we laughed. He cried and we spun into action. On the day of this memory, family members and I were visiting a lush, scenic park. We were sitting cross-legged in a loose circle admiring—guess who?—the curly-headed wonder who was performing antics in the middle. He was the actor, and we were the audience. But he had no idea that he was in the spotlight. He was too busy testing himself and forcing his little legs forward.

All was well—until. . . . Suddenly, his unstable legs decided that they could no longer support his weight. He started to sway. His body teetered back and forth, side to side, halfway down, up again, and then—boom! He was on the ground. He landed right on his ample, diapered bottom. Well, we, his admirers, reacted as if his fall was entertainment. We giggled, we laughed, and we exclaimed "Aaah!" What was his 14-month-old response to our amusement? He was mortified!

He looked at me, his mom, with round, horror-stricken eyes. The expression on his frozen face begged me to help him. He clumsily and hurriedly made his way to my lap and buried his head there, hoping he could disappear and escape the laughter and attention.

I was startled. Up to that point, it had never occurred to me that a child of that age could experience humiliation. But in that moment, looking into those eyes, reading his expression, I knew the shame was real.

On that day, my son learned that after a little maternal cuddling and a temporary move to a quieter and more isolated spot, he needed to get back on that horse and continue plodding forward. I learned something, too. I learned that children—even very young children—are fully equipped with a full range of human emotions. And no matter how much you love them and try to protect them, they are vulnerable to embarrassment and humiliation.

The message I took away from this incident helped me deal with a potential humiliating situation that involved my second son. During his elementary school years, this son developed a nervous habit that included a shaking of his hand (as if he were trying to force a bug off) and a jerking of his head (as if he were looking behind him to see if anything was there). I wondered, "Could it be normal development for him? An extra dose of nervous energy? A mild form of some clinical disorder?" I didn't know the answers to these questions. But I did know this: It was important for kids his age to fit in.

No matter how likeable you are in elementary school, a jerking head and a shaking hand can be a social challenge, one I preferred he avoided, if possible. I did not want to humiliate my son privately or publicly, so I waited patiently for the right moment to handle this *sensitively*. As I watched and waited, time went on, and so did the jerking and the shaking. I decided to make light of the behavior and to incorporate a sense of humor.

One day, I watched him playing ball outside with a group of friends. And his hand was shaking and his head was jerking. When he came home, I told him how much I had enjoyed watching him fully engaged in his outdoor activities. Then I added, lightly and humorously, "I saw you do this (acting out the shaking) and I saw you do this (acting out the jerking)." He looked at me aghast. When he saw what his behaviors looked like when I sported them, they lost their attractiveness and comfort. He stopped the behaviors immediately, and they never resurfaced again.

I am not saying that we solved any underlying anxieties here, but my son was fortunate. His condition was such that he was able to control his shaking behavior. I realize that there are other children with other conditions who cannot restrain their behavior, no matter how comforting, sensitive, or humorous their parents are. But in my son's case, we were able to help him ease his way into healthy social relationships. The lesson for our family was to handle this type of child-rearing issue gently and privately. If I had confronted him publicly or seriously, the tension he already carried may have increased, and that could have lead to a host of other challenges.

Then there is self-imposed humiliation. My daughter sentenced *herself* to this form of anguish. When she reached "that age," she, like many of her peers, did not wish to admit she had parents. We, as it turned out, *were* the humiliation. We didn't have to do much. I am sure our very existence was the problem. My independent daughter's discomfort cropped up when she started to establish her own adolescent identity. I considered her actions a comical variation of some type of teenage separation anxiety. A note to playful parents: It is easy to tease children who are in this mode. My husband and I discovered that all you have to do is go talk to their friends.

My daughter was active in a variety of school activities, so my husband and I were always, it seemed, watching and celebrating the culmination of some group effort. After the various performances and ceremonies, we did what we always did—we socialized. Since kids are people too, we were told, we talked to my daughter's friends. As her peers conversed with us, delighting in our compliments and attention, she would throw us darts, agonized looks, and lots of sighs (those of the female persuasion can be *very* dramatic). On the way home, we would be the amused recipients of teenage attitude.

Fortunately, with time and independence, my daughter was able to outgrow this phase. One day, after several years of maturation, she admitted how mortified she had been when her dad and I talked to her friends. It took her a while to realize that her friends actually enjoyed talking with us. In fact, they seemed to like us. When the clouds in her developing mind parted and the sun was able to shine through, it became apparent to her that we might actually have been an asset instead of a self-imposed humiliation.

Private and public humiliation can have a devastating effect on children. Stuttering is a good example. I have seen parents try to disgrace their children into verbal fluency because they desperately wanted to avoid the pain of having a permanent stutterer who would, no doubt, be teased at school. For some children, stuttering is a temporary stage of language development. For others, it is a long or even lifetime challenge.

When my children began their relationship with speech, the words fell out of their mouths haltingly and repetitively. Even though I was too new at parenting to know for sure, I suspected this was a natural phase of language development. As a result, my decision was to ignore it. I decided not to fill in the words my kids were searching for. I let them struggle and I watched them overcome. Their speech faltered and sputtered as their brains searched for new ways to create sounds. But I gave them my full attention, just as I would any other person who was talking to me. I responded with the appropriate nonverbal messages to validate that I was interested—a nod of the head, an "uh-huh," and direct eye contact. When they got the message that there was nothing unusual in their effort, their speech soon began to flow. Because I chose not to make stuttering an issue, because I never humiliated my kids about it, before I knew it, the behavior was gone. If I had attempted to shame them into accepted speech patterns prematurely, the end result very well could have been the opposite outcome I was looking for.

Who has not witnessed the humiliation some children suffer at the hands of their parents in groceries, retail shops, and restaurants? I understand that the goal of these parents—who are yelling, threatening, and bullying—is to teach their children to behave in a way that will not humiliate *them*, the parents, publicly. Parents know they are being judged in public settings. They take steps to demonstrate that they are actively "handling it" and are attempting to mold their children's behavior to fit society's expectations. But every time I see it and every time I hear it, I cringe.

As I watch "errant" children cower with warm, wet tears flowing down their cheeks, I envision my oldest son's baby face. I relive his embarrassment and his discomfort when he was a toddler who clumsily fell to the ground to the sound of laughter. I know these children feel humiliation as other shoppers gaze at them and their parents suspiciously.

My advice to parents in this situation is to take some extra time. Move your children outside. Explain how their behavior is affecting you and those around you. Keep them outside until they agree to go back in on your terms. Go home, if you have to. Do your time-outs. But whatever you decide to do, do it privately—for everyone's sake. Do not make the grocery a place of humiliation and disgrace for your children. Even though you may be able to teach them to sit quietly and attentively, they are paying a heavy price for the lesson.

Through their experiences, my children taught me to honor them by delicately correcting them outside of public viewing. From their real-life examples, I learned that whether a humiliating situation was self-imposed or forced upon them from the outside, I needed to respond with patience and compassion, two qualities which, when combined, have the potential to help stop humiliation in its tracks and spare our children unnecessary pain.

HUMILITY

HUMILITY IS THE
EMBARRASSMENT YOU
FEEL WHEN YOU TELL
PEOPLE HOW WONDERFUL
YOU ARE.
–Laurence J. Peter

Humility is a remarkable thing. Out of all of the character traits I have witnessed, humility—which I define as a modest, unassuming, unpretentious nature—is the quality I admire most. Humble people quietly go about their business leading, creating, and succeeding for little reward—other than the joy they receive from the process. They have no hungry egos to feed. They do not blow their own horns or sing their own praises. In their lives, they conduct quiet, understated music that is rich and controlled. As a new mom, I thought to myself, "Raising humble children would be a blessing, indeed."

Many years ago, my husband and I made a new friend. We saw this person in a group setting several times over several months. We enjoyed his company—his sweetness, his gentleness, and his sense of humor. One day, through light, social conversation, someone else revealed to us that this man worked in a profession that is highly esteemed in our society. I remember being stunned. Why didn't he tell us? People who work in that field usually let us know within minutes what they do for a living and what their title is. And their revelation is often touched with a bit of arrogance and elitism—which can easily translate into social aloofness. I talked to my husband about the surprise disclosure the whole way home. I was impressed by a character trait that was carried so tenderly, that touched others so softly. I was awed by this man's humility.

I only had two of my three children at the time, but I knew then that humility was a quality I wanted to instill in these two siblings and in any future members of our brood. Humility spreads its sweet fragrance gracefully. As the aroma floats, it influences those who come in contact with it. Humility elicits wonder and admiration. It inspires those of us who recognize it to explore our own characters—to soul-search and to measure ourselves against it. Would my children rise to my "humble" expectations?

When it came to raising humble children, I had a head start. My husband is defined by this quality. His humility was dear to me the day I met him, and it is just as dear to me today. I had a wonderful example living in my own home. How fortunate! Good choosing on my part! It seems that humility is a trait I (and many others) am magnetically drawn to.

If you ask my children today how they believe humility was instilled in their developing personalities, I bet you they would say something like this: "In addition to our parents' role modeling, we were gently and consistently reminded that we were not the center of the universe, that the world did not revolve around our desires, that we were part of a family group, and that everyone's needs were important—*even mom's and dad's.*" They would go on to say that each member of the family was special, but no one member was better than any other.

Many examples of humility-instilling opportunities arose in our household. Talking on the telephone is an example every parent can relate to. I remember talking on the phone with a dear friend. We were happily catching up. "How are the kids?

Did Johnny get the lead in the play he was auditioning for? How is Jennifer feeling about the big gymnastics event coming up?" I remember being engrossed in my conversation and enjoying the comfortable interaction and the mutual sharing.

When I was at the peak of my involvement, my children advanced—like swarming bees humming toward a honey pot or, if you prefer, like moths drifting toward a lonely evening glow. My children were earnest in their efforts to interrupt me. They seemed to be acting under pure "worker bee" instinct. "Mom, can I . . . ." "Mom, I need . . . ." I am sure you parents know the script.

It seemed that even though my little "bees" had easily learned other rules of etiquette (like knocking before entering someone's room), they had trouble conquering the urge to wait until their mother was finished with her telephone conversation.

When my children were young and learning to define their roles in our family structure, it was necessary for me to interrupt my phone conversation *momentarily* to let my kids know that their intrusion was not acceptable. This was done with a quick "Excuse me, please," to the voice at the other end of the line, and then a quick "I am on the phone. You cannot talk to me right now," to the kids. I used a serious, firm voice that emanated from a stern, hardened face. Accompanying my words was a purposeful arm gesture directing my children to cease and desist *immediately*. I made it clear that I would not be addressing any of their intrusions while I was talking on the phone—and I never did. If they were being extra hyper or demanding, I suggested that they write down their message so that they could remember it and communicate it to me after I hung up.

When I was off the phone, my children got a "talking to." My words included temperate reminders that reinforced the lessons I mentioned above: 1) you are not the center of the universe; 2) the world does not revolve around you; 3) you are part of a family group; and 4) we are all important, and we all have needs. I did not communicate my sentiments harshly. I tenderly talked about respect—for me, my friend, and our time. I included the frustration my friend and I felt when our conversation was rudely interrupted. After all, he or she may have been seeking a sympathetic ear or some good advice.

My discourse was always reinforced with direct eye contact, a controlled voice, and physical touch—such as my hand resting on the child's shoulder or arm.

The next time my children tried the same "interrupt-Mom" trick as a way of testing me to see if I meant what I said earlier, the result was magical. I no longer had to interrupt my conversation. I no longer had to use my controlled voice. This time my communication was completely nonverbal. I gave the look and flashed the gesturing arm. Their reactions? Sad faces (defeat) and about-faces (win for my team). Pretty soon, all it took was the look in my eyes. And soon after that, they didn't even dream of interrupting my phone conversations. They chose to wait it out and avoid the drama. They quickly learned that they were not going to wear me down over time and that my needs were just as important as theirs.

Of course, as often happens with children, a lesson can turn right back on you. Nothing is predictable in child rearing. And one day the humility lesson boomeranged to me.

My husband and I had a party at our home. We invited lots of friends and family. The adults were cheerful and social. The children were occupied and amused. My middle son appeared at my side, huffing and puffing. He was wearing the rosy cheeks of someone who had been hanging upside down on a jungle gym.

"Mom!" he said.

"I am talking," I responded.

"But Mom," he continued.

I insisted that my time be respected.

He tried one more time. Then, defeated, he sadly shrugged his shoulders, turned his back, and walked away.

A few minutes later, when I was done with my conversation, I sought him out to see what he wanted. Well, apparently, this was the day *I* was supposed to learn a lesson. My son was in the backyard, and this is what I saw: My "interrupting son" was hovering over his little sister, who was twisted and tangled in a swing and hanging upside down. Her hair was knotted as gravity pulled her twisted curls down, down, down. Her cheeks were bright red with blood flow. But she was quiet—because her brother had taken it upon himself to be her temporary parent, to take my place as I stubbornly insisted on finishing my conversation. He soothed her. He stayed by her side.

I was horrified—at her situation *and* at my handling of it. This was something I did not foresee. But I admired my son, and I was grateful for his vigilant attendance to his dangling little sister.

So we had a family talk. We discussed emergencies. We spoke about times when it was not only appropriate but absolutely necessary for parents to be interrupted.

I started off trying to teach humility to my children, and what did I get? A big piece of humble pie that tasted something like this: *I* am not the center of the universe. The world does not revolve around *me*. I am *one* member of a wonderful family unit, and we are *all* important—*even my children*!

So now that I am at the end of this chapter, I realize that humility is more than a modest, unassuming, unpretentious nature, as I defined it at the beginning of this section. Humility also incorporates a polite respect for others—what they say, what they do, and what they feel. I am proud of my three humble children. Because they don't conduct their lives from an ego-driven posture, they glide smoothly from one place to another. They are as attentive to the local waiter or grocery clerk as they are to the most esteemed professional or corporate head. I could go on and on and brag about my kids' unassuming natures and their courteous respect for others, but that just wouldn't be humble now, would it?

I'M SORRY

AN APOLOGY IS SAYING
THE RIGHT THING
AFTER DOING THE
WRONG THING.

"Love means never having to say you're sorry." I have heard that phrase many times, from many faces, in many places. And I think it's foolish! I have adopted a different philosophy: If I do something wrong or hurt someone, I say, "I'm sorry"—*especially* if it's someone I love, and even if that someone is younger than I am (like one of my children, for example). My viewpoint is simple, and it has worked well for me. Rather than defend myself, I apologized after I made a parental blunder. Almost immediately, my children respected my expression of contrition. That respect replaced the frustration and anger that had been hovering in the air.

My mother adopted the phrase "Love means *never* having to say you're sorry" after watching the movie *Love Story*. She felt that *not* saying "I'm sorry" was an expression of deep, abiding love, a love in which you were completely understood without ever uttering a word. I was very frustrated by her easy embrace of that philosophy. It never rang true to me. Yes, I was *just* a kid, but I was still a member of the human race, and I felt that that affiliation alone deserved some level of appreciation—a simple "I'm sorry" when appropriate. Even worse for me than the missing apology was the silent treatment that often replaced what should have been an easy statement of regret.

I have seen many other people integrate my mother's philosophy into their lifestyles and into their child-rearing practices. I always cringed when I saw it applied. And I always questioned its motive. Have these parents decided not to say "I'm sorry" because of their deep, abiding love for their children? Or are these parents not saying "I'm sorry" because their ego is in the way and they are afraid of losing their stature and standing in the eyes of their offspring?

I remember once sitting across the dinner table from a newly married couple. The "newbie" husband pushed back from the table and awkwardly attempted to rise from his chair. As he did so, one leg of his chair landed squarely on the foot of his loved one. She let out a yelp, and he let out a reprimand. Yes, a reprimand. Why? Well, her foot had the audacity to find its way to the bottom of his chair leg. In his mind the incident was obviously her fault, which meant that she deserved no apology or concern from him. I was astounded by his reaction. The first year of marriage is normally filled with expressions of kindness and love. So how could this new groom be so insensitive to his bride's suffering? Did he also see the movie *Love Story*? Did he also choose to adopt its philosophy? Or was he embarrassed by his inelegant moves and more concerned about his clumsy image than he was about his wife's pain?

After working my way through many family sagas, I have discovered this: It is best to have *no* ego when relating to the people you love. *That* is how you build stature. *That* is how you earn respect. My children have heard me apologize many times. And each and every time, I meant it.

Did I pick them up late? "I'm sorry." Yes, I may have had a crazy, frenzied day. But the moment I apologized, I acknowledged to my children that their time was every bit as precious as mine.

After my apology, I made amends, if appropriate. If they missed 10 minutes of play time here, I gave them 10 extra minutes of reading time there.

Did I say something personal, something that embarrassed my kids in front of their friends? "I'm *very* sorry." I was probably carried away with the conversation of the moment. Without thinking of the effect my words would have, I revealed something that my kids felt was private or outdated. How insensitive of me. I traded a couple of minutes of attention and laughs (my ego) for a breach of my children's privacy. This one couldn't be solved with 10 minutes of extra play time. But I did *sincerely* apologize to my children. I assured them that in the future I would be thinking before speaking and that I would, indeed, protect their privacy. I let my children know that I am not too old to learn new tricks and that I will become a better and more trustworthy parent because of this episode.

I have a lot of respect for people who are comfortable enough in their own skin to apologize to others, when appropriate. It takes a big person to admit that he has goofed, take responsibility for the blunder, and be willing to make amends. And it takes an even bigger person to acknowledge that other people's feelings are important too. There is a lesson here about communication as well: Express your feelings of remorse and your feelings of contrition. *Do not assume that the person you have hurt, even if they love you, feels your silent regret.* Most of us are *not* telepathic. We cannot read the minds of our loved ones—and they certainly can't read ours.

The more I have apologized to my loved ones, the more I have been honored, respected, and trusted by them. The more I have apologized to my loved ones, the more they have been able to relate to me as a vulnerable human being who is willing to atone for my mistakes and learn from them. How do I know this is true? Because I have seen it on my children's faces.

I remember once "having it out" with my daughter. I said some things that were unfair, and she responded with hurt and anger. After we gave each other some space, *I went to her* and apologized for my unmerited statements. I also pointed out her part in the episode. As I exposed myself, her eyes went from tight with fear and upset to open with wonder and relief. Her tense body began to relax. She realized this was not going to be a power struggle. She was not going to have to defend herself. She was going to be honored with an apology. The next two things out of her mouth were an acknowledgement of her contribution and an apology for her behavior. We both smiled. We both hugged. We both learned something. Each episode thereafter became easier and easier for us to deal with. Eventually, our exchanges developed into a fluid dance that mother and daughter performed gracefully. Apologies remove defensiveness and turn potential arguments into open and honest communication.

When I learned to say "I'm sorry," my kids learned to say it too—rather than defend themselves at all costs. The words "I'm sorry" bestow honor, respect, and trust on the receiver. They also boomerang honor, respect, and trust to the speaker. When I strengthened my "I'm sorry" with amends, I developed a winning combination for our family.

Holding the title of parent didn't mean I automatically knew how to handle every child-rearing issue. New scenarios and new challenges popped into our lives every day. I had to think on my feet and make instantaneous decisions regarding the health, welfare, and safety of my children. I did not "get it right" each and every time. Often I made mistakes. When I did, I admitted them to my children. As I learned from my missteps, my children learned from my role modeling. They clearly comprehended that *egos are not above doing the right thing*.

There were other lessons gleaned from this philosophy as well:

I learned *not* to speak when I was feeling exhausted and testy. Instead, I separated myself from my loved ones. I went into a dark room, took deep breaths, repeated affirmations, did yoga stretches—whatever worked for me that day. In this way, I learned *not* to set myself up for a future apology. I knew my limits, and I understood that I had the power to inflict pain on my loved ones. This separation behavior taught me volumes about self-control. This was a lesson I was able to pass on to my children as well.

Further, I learned that defending myself at all costs often made me look stubborn, illogical, and ridiculous. Is the person who is obstinate and irrational worthy of respect? Or is the person who admits he or she is obstinate and irrational worthy of respect? Another great lesson that my children absorbed.

So here is my philosophy in a nutshell: Love means *always* saying "I'm sorry" when you make a mistake or hurt someone. Don't let your ego and vulnerabilities keep you from earning the respect of your loved ones or interrupt the flow of communication you enjoy with your spouse and children. Yes, self-image is important, but only if it chooses to sacrifice itself to justice and fairness when appropriate. Weaknesses can be revealed without giving anything up, if they are exposed openly and honestly to those you love. Don't habitually defend and protect yourself. Explanations are good, but excuses are not. Hear the other side. Own up. Apologize. Make amends. Doing so reduces the tension in the household by making everyone feel like they are a valuable member of the family.

This philosophy applies to spousal relationships as well. The most effective parents work as a unified team. Members of the team must be able to respect and trust each other and feel safe enough to communicate their feelings and perspectives openly. A simple apology can help move two sides of an opposing viewpoint to a cohesive and loving center. When parents can communicate honestly and express regret comfortably, the kids end up being the winners. The children in these families are able to enjoy time in a home that is free of power-grabbing egos, devoid of defensive tension, and replete with admiration for other members of the family. They begin to feel secure, and they learn to take responsibility for their actions.

So instead of seeing a movie about never having to say you're sorry, I would like to see a movie about saying you're sorry when it's appropriate. Such a movie would encourage healthy emotional risk taking, enrich family relationships, and make a contribution to peace and harmony among loved ones. And the bonus is that people who are happy and secure within their family units have a greater chance of mushrooming those positive feelings to the world at large.

 LETTING GO

> THE TROUBLE WITH THE
> FAMILY IS THAT CHILDREN
> GROW OUT OF
> CHILDHOOD, BUT PARENTS
> NEVER GROW OUT OF
> PARENTHOOD.
> —OSHO

From the first moment my children announced their presence into the world, I knew one thing for certain: I was raising my kids in order to let them go. I was a temporary custodian, caregiver, and teacher, but I was *not* the owner of a delightful piece of property; nor was I the master over a tiny likeness of me. My children did not enter my life in order to fill my needs. I was there to fill theirs—to feed, clothe, care for, and supervise them—and to back off when appropriate. My job was to prepare them to make their own decisions, watch them enjoy or suffer the consequences, give them age-appropriate freedoms, and observe how they handled the gift. My job was *not* to spare them pain or to make things easy. It was *not* to control the details of their lives. On the contrary, my task was to encourage them to learn to manage themselves.

My daughter called me the other day, and we had such a nice conversation. We had a wonderful time discussing impending midterm exams and papers, an inspiring professor who communicates with wit and charm, and her plans for the future. At the end of the conversation, my daughter said cheerfully, "See you in a month, Mom." It struck me at that moment how healthy my letting-go philosophy was. As my life continued to unfold, that happy little voice on the other end of the phone came back to me. It validated my philosophy and rewarded me. I felt proud that my daughter and her brothers were handling their lives so successfully and proud that I encouraged them to do so.

I have watched friends and acquaintances as their children left the nest, and I have noticed that it is harder for some than for others. Some parents appear lost, sensing a hole of enormous proportions in the fabric of their lives, one that they have no idea how to repair. Others grieve, with tears and sadness, not knowing how to fill the void. And others, like me, contentedly assist their fledglings out of the nest and delight at their developing ability to fly. Why am I not torturing myself over my empty nest? I have shifted my focus from child rearing to numerous other endeavors and activities. One of the *many* pieces of my pie is my close relationship with my children. My children do not comprise my whole pie.

And I have watched the children of other parents as well. Some high school graduates were fearful to separate, so they stayed in or near their parents' home, and they made life choices that enabled them to continue to do so. Other high school graduates bravely took flight, but within a semester or two were home again, comfortable in the knowledge that the buck no longer stopped with them; it stopped with their parents, again. And then there were still others, like my children, who bravely and cheerfully waved good-bye as their choices lead them to other cities, states, and countries.

I am a big fan of junior colleges, vocational institutions, and work experience, but my hope for my children was that they would make their decisions based upon their abilities and interests, not on geography and separation anxiety. I am not saying that an out-of-town college education is better than a local one or that a four-year institution is better than a two-year. What I am saying is that my children were able to take full advantage of *all* of their options—two-year college, vocational college, four-year college, out-of state college, work experience—and choose whichever one best suited their goals. I am happy to report that they took on their new challenges eagerly. They were ready, willing, and able to jump new hurdles. They rushed ahead full steam, prepared to learn their life lessons and to develop their budding characters.

Often, puzzled parents asked me about my relationship with my children. Why aren't you miserable? Are you close to your children? How many times a week do you call them? I find myself stuttering through my answers. I consider my children and I to be very close. But I can't prove that by how many times I call them or they call me. My definition of "closeness" does not include a tally of phone calls and e-mail messages. So I shyly and hesitatingly respond, "Yes, we are close. But, no, I really don't call my children often." Or, "They call me when they have something to share."

Many parents have proudly announced to me that they call their college students every day. And many grown children have groaned to me that their parents call them *all day long*. One parent was proud to inform me that she called her college daughter every morning to wake her up and make sure she made it to her first class on time. And I have heard from my own children about other moms who traveled long distances to spend a weekend with their college-age children, attend Saturday-night parties with them, and supply the beer. When I queried my kids about the reaction of their peers to the visiting party moms (who dressed like college students in order to fit in), I was told that, more often than not, the students felt uncomfortable around them.

In contrast, I call my children when I have something to share, and they call me for the same reason. No one keeps track of numbers or times. If my husband and I travel to visit one of our children in a distant town, we enjoy their company during the day and give them their Saturday night to be with friends— unless of course, they tell us that they would prefer to "hang" with us, which often happens.

So what is my definition of closeness? Well, let's look at the content of some of the conversations I do have with my children. Here is what they are *not*: What did you do at 8 o'clock, 9 o'clock, and 10 o'clock? Do you miss me? I think you should take this class, that class, or the other. I think you should do this, that, or the other. Are you eating any vegetables? How long has it been since you washed your sheets?

Here is what they *are*. Mom, you would be so proud of me. I have been invited to join this program. Out of thousands of applicants, they chose me. Let's talk about it. I would like your opinion. Or, Mom, you would be so proud of me. I just came back from a conference where I presented my research, and it was a big success. Let me tell you the direction I have decided to take this. I would like your opinion. Or, Mom, you would be so proud of me. I took a chance on this paper and told the professor exactly what I think, even though it was contrary to his theories. And guess what? He loved it. Let me read you these paragraphs. I would like your opinion. Or, Mom, you would be so proud of me. This obstacle and that obstacle were thrown into my path. This is how I chose to handle the situation. The results were even better than I had imagined. Let me tell you about it. I would like your opinion.

My children and I are close because we share ideas, not because we keep track of time. I give my children the freedom *not* to call me, and they, in turn, give me the gift of their accomplishments and opinions—whenever they occur. If my children sleep late and miss a class or an hour of work, it is their responsibility to bear, and the consequences are theirs to learn from. Their last-minute, mad-dash panic is going to teach them to get up with the alarm clock next time. It is *not* my job to thrust myself into my children's lives on a daily basis. As I have quietly and patiently focused on my own life, my children have happily and willingly invited me into theirs.

As I step backward and let my children control their lives, I also step forward and begin managing mine. I have discovered that this "empty-nest" phase of life is a thrilling one for me. Because I am rekindling old interests and discovering so many new ones, I feel fulfilled with my life. As a result, I am able to let my children go. An "empty nest" need not be empty. It can easily be filled with a variety of activities, pursuits, and interests. I feel that I am living my life fully. I am expanding my culinary skills and stimulating my palate on a regular basis. The music floating through the rooms of my home is music that fills *my* soul. My days extend beyond my work and home. They include projects, crafts, artistic expression, physical activity, self-didactic learning, entrepreneurship, and community involvement. The uninterrupted time I spend with my husband has brought us closer together than ever before. After many dedicated years, I am free of the daily entanglements of child rearing and am directing my own life. This is *a gift to my children*. While they are out slaying their dragons, they need not worry one bit about how their mom is doing.

My children delight in the fact that they are *not* the center of my universe. My daughter recently told me that she is grateful for the freedom she has to develop as an individual, eccentricities and all. She expressed it this way, "Thank God you are not one of *those* moms. I couldn't have survived. Thank you for letting me handle this my way." One of my sons recently expressed that he was very pleased to hear about my involvement in a particular project. He felt I was alight with the joy of it. And my other son expressed that he is proud to introduce my husband and me to his friends and acquaintances whenever he is able to do so.

My life is full, and my children enjoy that. They do not carry the burden of making me feel whole or filling my empty spaces. They are busy living their lives, making their choices, and sharing, when they choose, their newly acquired wisdom and experience with me.

And here is the bonus. My house is so neat! No flip-flops in the entryway. No unicycles in the den. No water polo balls in the living room. No water bottles on the couch. No backpacks on the kitchen counter. No books on the floor. Life is good.

So in answer to the question, "Are you close to your children?" my answer is, "Yes, we are close." Do we talk to each other every day? No, we don't. But from my point of view, time and distance do not make closeness. Closeness is that bit of news that doesn't seem real or complete until you share it with your mom and dad and get their enthusiastic backing and support. It is that recent accomplishment that you can't wait to disclose. It is the depth of the conversations you have. It is the wisdom that is gained and imparted (which goes both ways, by the way). It is the opinions that are sought but, after careful consideration, are not always followed (and that's okay).

As I go about living my life, I feel very close to my children. And the closeness only grows with the silence that fills the spaces between our conversations. Our closeness is solid and concrete. It's not going anywhere. It is not needy. It does not have to be proven by "x" number of conversations within "x" amount of time. My children's lives are full, and my life is complete. Our independence defines our closeness.

Because this approach has worked successfully for me, I urge other parents to consider refilling their nests— for themselves this time around. My nest is not empty. It just has new eggs. I have invited projects, friendships, involvement, and learning into my nest. I have taken the advice I have given to my kids so many times before: I have spread my wings high above and well beyond my family's nest, and I have been brave enough to jump into new challenges and adventures.

# MOVIES

Sit down. Grab a bowl of popcorn, and prepare yourself. I know I have a movie philosophy for child rearing that is, most likely, different from your own. When I explain it to other parents, who are working so hard to protect the innocence of their children and teach them good values, I usually get raised eyebrows, dropped jaws, and general surprise as a response.

Here we go: My children were allowed (and often encouraged) to see R-rated movies.

Now, take a breath and let me clarify. My children were allowed to see *good* R-rated movies (starting at an age at which they could understand and discuss the concepts involved). What is my definition of a good R-rated movie? One that teaches an honest lesson about life, one that weaves values into its story line, one that celebrates the victory of good over evil, or one that engenders lively discussion and an exchange of ideas—whether I agreed with the viewpoints or not.

Part of my job as a parent was to teach my children how to think. And I found movies to be an invaluable tool. They were easily accessible and inexpensive, and my children were eager to participate. I risked exposing my children to some four-letter words, to some nudity, and to some depictions of unhealthy lifestyles in order to accomplish my goal of raising children who could think through tough issues and maneuver themselves safely through difficult situations.

My husband and I accompanied our children to these R-rated films, 1) because, by law, they had to be accompanied by an adult, 2) because none of their friends' parents would take them, and 3) because mom and dad would be right there when the film ended to answer questions and discuss certain scenes that were depicted—usually over chips and salsa at our favorite Mexican restaurant. Since we saw lots of movies, we ate lots of Mexican food. We had our own table at our favorite south-of-the-border retreat. It had a nice, circular shape, which made it easy for us to search each others' eyes during our deep "round-table" discussions.

How could I have denied my children the opportunity to see *Schindler's List*, for example, a movie about the wickedness that was the Holocaust and one man's efforts, at his own personal risk, to save the lives of strangers? This movie, more than almost any other, supported my motivation for taking the time to write this chapter. Believe me, I would rather be sleeping at 5 a.m. than writing about mass slaughter. But how could I have passed up this cinematographic opportunity to share with my children the depth of human evil—how to recognize it, how to fight it (in yourself and others), and how to understand the consequences? How could I have missed the opportunity to teach my children about this genocidal time in history and to instill empathy in them for the innocent victims? And how could I have denied myself the opportunity to instruct them on the importance of being good, kind, and empathetic, and on the many ways *society* benefits when children are raised to exhibit those qualities?

After we left this movie, the discussion we had at the "round table" was quieter than usual. It was more subdued. There was sadness weighing down the spicy aroma of our combination plates. But through the melancholy, my husband and I were able to lead our children in a dialogue about how an evil Nazi guard trying fervently to impress his superiors and rise in the SS hierarchy had the power to affect millions of innocent people. We also talked about the goodness of individuals, like Oskar Schindler, who risked their lives to provide care and assistance to the troubled souls of the region. I am grateful that Steven Spielberg granted me a vehicle through which I could discuss these important issues with my children.

How about the movie *Shine*? Here we have a biographical story of pianist David Helfgott and how he overcame very challenging odds. As a child, he suffered from an oppressive, intimidating father. The film goes on to describe Helfgott's musical brilliance, his battle with schizophrenia, his fixating passion for music, and his eventual triumph. This movie was a gift to me for my children. How better to teach them about overcoming life's obstacles? Here was a man who, through steadfastness and inner strength, was able to orchestrate living, breathing, musical victories from the many half notes and quarter notes he was dealt. This movie was an inspiration to my children, who were facing daily challenges from friends, teachers, and societal rules. If David Helfgott had the courage to confront his substantial demons, so too could they face their childhood frustrations and annoyances.

There are so many R-rated movies that I supported as vehicles for a lively exchange of ideas. *Higher Learning* focused our family's attention on anger and prejudice on college campuses. This movie was fertile ground on which to discuss arming yourself against hatred, loathing, and peer pressure; the importance of knowing who you are, confidently and unassailably; and using that knowledge as a source of strength when confronted with coercion from the outside.

Shakespeare in Love was the perfect vehicle through which I could expose my children to the inventiveness of a superior romance comedy. As the movie's bard weaved himself through the tragic tale of *Romeo and Juliet*, my family could reach back into history and learn about another time, another place, another form of expression, and the all-consuming nature of love.

Glory introduced my children to injustice and the horrors of war. But it also launched them into a story of honor, bravery, and commitment. This movie ignited discussions about how much you are willing to risk, and what you are willing to risk it for. It raised questions about overcoming fear and dedicating yourself to a cause.

Good Will Hunting offered us a conduit though which we could explore innate talents waiting to be discovered. Our family was able to explore whether institutionalized learning is enough. Emotional expression, interaction with others, and a desire to reach your potential all contribute to a successful life.

Shawshank Redemption consumed us with its themes of maintaining hope under grueling circumstances, the value of freedom, and the thrill of redemption.

Movie time offered my family a lot of rewarding conversation. We threw out ideas, we observed how and if they were accepted, and we measured whether they withstood lively and enthusiastic challenges. The children got very skilled at formulating original points of view, defending them, and testing their theories on others, just like they did during our family's dinnertime conversations. They even became adept at playing the devil's advocate by ardently supporting an opposing perspective in order to rile up their parents or sharpen their skills.

These mental movie exercises shaped my children in many ways. My kids learned to give birth to new concepts and to risk communicating them openly. They learned that when presented with a formula of facts, they were able to create a textbook of conclusions. They learned to integrate issues of honor and moral values into their character. Movie sessions conducted in a safe learning environment taught my children how to reflect on important issues and formulate ideas. Their courageous participation at these meetings helped prepare them to navigate the stormy waters of middle school, high school, college, and beyond.

R-rated movies, with parental guidance and instruction, have contributed more to my children's character than yet another silly summer show. Yet I understand that parents must decide for themselves if the themes and images presented in these movies are likely to enhance or detract from their character-building responsibilities. When we felt our children could handle it and learn from it (despite some nudity here and some foul language there), we took them. Today, they routinely call us and advise us of movies they want us to see. Why? Because they still want to discuss the subject matter and their opinions with us.

When I was raising my children, I read movie reviews carefully. I researched themes and issues. I decided whether my children could benefit from viewing and discussing a movie's difficult challenges or uplifting highlights—even if it was rated R. Only after I had done *my* work, did my family hop in the car to share some movie time. But the movie was only part of a fuller experience. The Mexican restaurant—the discussions, the sharing, and the challenges—was where the real value of a movie was determined.

MUSIC

AFTER SILENCE, THAT
WHICH COMES NEAREST
TO EXPRESSING THE
INEXPRESSIBLE IS MUSIC.
−Aldous Huxley

Music is powerful. It unites. It
excites. It soothes. I didn't always understand the potential
music has to enhance our lives. My children taught me about
the allure of music, each in their own way. Their love of this
magnificent art shaped my thinking with regard to certain child-
rearing issues. Here are some of the things I pondered when my
children were young: Should my kids have music on when they
are studying? If music does enter their homework space, do I
insist on soft, understated background melodies, or do I let the
kids decide? And what about objectionable lyrics?

Like many other parents, I had heard about studies that
claimed that children who engage in musical activities perform
better academically than those who don't. It was in my children's
best interest, it seemed, to develop a love of music. I opened my
ears to their musical choices, and then I sat back and observed
their behavior. Music created enchantment—a free flow of
thought and energy. It reduced stress levels and encouraged

creativity. Music helped my children perform at their scholastic best. But I had to keep an open mind in order for their music to weave its spell. I had to accept that my children were doing their schoolwork to music. And I had to recognize that the music they chose helped them to focus on their tasks.

My first musical challenge was Son Number One. When I walked into his room during afterschool hours, this kid was sitting in a straight-back chair that was pulled up to a sturdy desk that housed a sensible lamp. So far so good. This is how I was raised, and it was what I expected from my children. But there was more. I heard music—loud, blasting, and assaulting—pounding the walls of his room. My first thought was alarm: "Homework should be performed in a quiet setting, someplace akin to a library. Son Number One needs complete silence in order to focus on his mathematical tables and his who-do-I-admire-most writing assignment." And I told him so. But he was not buying my argument. Son Number One disagreed—vehemently.

He enlightened me with his logic. It seemed the music helped him concentrate. It put him in just the right "groove." And the proof? How could I argue with the fact that his grades were so good?

It was time for me to step back and reconsider. Could it actually be that the music helped him concentrate? That thought ran counter to everything I had been taught about study space. But the music kept him in his chair. It helped him complete his homework assignments, consistently and on time. He required no pressure from me. And then there were those grades.

My son and I made a deal: He could keep the musical status quo while I observed and researched the results. The outcome was that the music never did come down or off, and the grades kept coming in. This is what I concluded: Don't mess with something that is obviously working. Let him study with his music on. Let the "sleeping boy" lie.

Next came Son Number Two. He also studied surrounded by the beat of many musical drummers. I was accustomed to that by now. But there was something new. Son Number Two offered a further parental challenge. In addition to studying while listening to music, he tested me further by reading his assignments hanging upside down from the living room couch. This propelled me into even more serious contemplation. No private room? No chair? No desk? No cute little lamp? No perfect posture? How far can a mom stretch?

Since Son Number Two worked harder than most as he struggled to overcome a learning disability, and since I had already learned the musical lesson "if it works, don't change it" from Son Number One, I decided not to add stress to my second son's academic life. I put a smile on my face. I gave him a good-natured chuckle and a lighthearted pat on the foot, which was extending skyward at the time. Then I left him alone to study on his head. (I wonder if this behavior had anything to do with his interest in studying chimpanzees at one point in his life.) The grades kept coming in, and I decided to let the "suspended boy" lie.

Then came Child Number Three, my daughter. By the time she grew to homework age, I had learned to be open to the concept of music with study, and to the additional upside-down trimmings. My daughter and I never had one conversation about it. You want to blast the music while you are doing your homework? Fine. You want to blast the music, do your homework, and talk on the phone? Fine. You want to blast the music, do your homework, talk on the phone, and instant message your friends while you are filing your fingernails? Fine. This girl was a multitasker. She had trouble concentrating if she wasn't doing five things at once. The grades kept coming in. So I decided to let the "busy girl" lie.

My children's love of music inspired me to open myself to the idea of many nontraditional forms of study. I realized that different children concentrate and learn differently. Some can focus more easily with soft melodies floating in the background, and others prefer loud lyrics pounding the walls. Some shine when they are studying head down, and others excel when they are taking on multiple tasks simultaneously. I realized that as long as the work was being done and the grades were coming in, my job was easy. Let it all lie. Let my children have the freedom to formulate a study environment that worked for them.

Now, to the topic of popular lyrics. I never reacted harshly to "objectionable" lyrics being played in my home. My children were involved in music for the art of it, not for the shock of it. If it happened once or twice that one of my kids dabbled in lyrics my husband and I heard and found disturbing, we told them that those lyrics were offensive to us and that we did not want to hear them.

Because I never said, "You can't listen to this" but said, instead, "You can't listen to this *around me*," music was never used as a tool of rebellion by my children. But it was sometimes used as a key to unlock and release complicated feelings. My daughter told me that angry lyrics *never* bred angry thoughts in her or angry behavior, but, rather, liberated preexisting fury and frustration. She assured me that angry lyrics did *not* inspire her to think bad thoughts. Instead, when she was upset, they helped free her from trapped and troubled emotions.

I learned from my children that there is more to music than lyrics alone. Sometimes the beat of a song speaks to a raw emotional spot. My daughter admitted that many of the kids she knew didn't even know the words to the songs they were listening to. The importance of the music to them was the underlying tone, which seemed to touch a variety of emotional chords. I learned that I could predict my daughter's mood by the musical notes flowing (or pounding) through her bedroom walls. If those notes were loud, throbbing, and defiant, I just kept her door closed and waited for the music to weave its magic spell, which it usually did. My daughter used music as a form of emotional expression (sometimes angry, sometimes loving, and sometimes whimsical). Today she continues to use it for that purpose as she responds emotionally to its beauty, passion, harmony, and structure.

My children adore music. All kinds of music. And they appreciate good musicianship. They learned it on their own—not from me or my husband. (In fact, we learned it from them.) I am grateful I gave my kids the freedom to make their own choices and develop their own tastes. They listen to classical music, ethnic music, fifties music, popular music, jazz music, and old classics like Ella Fitzgerald. They delight in discovering new groups and sharing them with me and each other.

Each of my children has pursued music in his or her own way. Son Number One loves to collect and dabble in a variety of instruments: piano, guitar, clarinet, and banjo. Son Number Two used his voice as an instrument. He sang in a chamber choir all through high school and college. He enjoys playing the piano and the guitar and has studied gamalan sitting cross-legged on the floor. My daughter sang and danced her way through high school, played piano for one of the school's show choirs, and also studied gamalan. To this day, they are all deeply involved in music.

Because of what I learned from my children about the inherent power of music, my husband and I were able to witness and appreciate a magical moment. While visiting New Orleans, we walked into a tiny jazz club called Donna's. After having a warm and interesting discussion with the owner about red beans and rice and the best hamburgers in the Quarter, the music began to flow. Immediately, I was mesmerized. A very unassuming young man named Evan Christopher started playing his clarinet. As he played, Donna's milieu was transformed. I listened intently as his slow, smooth sounds encircled me in a bubble of enchantment. I felt my excitement build as the tempo increased and the clarinet began its dialogue with the guitar. The musicians' eyes were locked on each other as the musical themes they created were hurled back and forth. Their bodies were overtaken by the task they were engaged in. They were engulfed by the music. The listeners were overwhelmed. We were frozen in wonder.

When the artists took their break, I talked to this clarinetistmagician. I asked him how he knew the clarinet was his instrument. He told me that he didn't find the clarinet. The clarinet found him. He started on the piano and was introduced to the clarinet in a school setting. "It was the mechanics," he said. "The mechanics of the clarinet made sense to me."

Because Evan Christopher kept an open mind about musical instruments, he was able to soar on his clarinet and cast a spell on me. Because my children kept an open mind about all types of music, they have been able to appreciate its influence and to inspire others with their enthusiasm. Because I kept an open mind about the impact of music, I was able to encourage my children to develop their love for this art, each in their own way. My children's devotion to music is deep and enduring. Their musical choices have influenced them and transformed me. I am glad I allowed them to navigate these waters on a personal level—blasting, hanging, and multitasking. I respected the hold music had on my children, and that respect encouraged their love to grow.

But does music create good kids? My children loved music and they were good children. In our family, music wielded a certain limited power. But it did *not* instill goodness or character in my developing children—their genes and environment did. Music had the ability to heal my kids when they were angry, calm them when they were tense, and enliven them when they were down. But I *never* confused a love of music with moral fiber and integrity. Music was the great enhancer. It offered my children a form of expression, a method of release, and an appreciation of creative spirit. But music is what music is, and it has its limitations. When I learned to understand music's influence—and its boundaries—it became an important and useful addition to our home.

OVERUSING "NO" (TO LITTLE ONES)

IF YOU MUST SAY NO,
DON'T SAY IT FORTISSIMO.

Saying "no" to your child can be appropriate and effective, especially when combined with a respectful explanation of why. "No. Don't run into the street. A car could hit you." Kids can handle "no" and benefit from the directness, especially if danger is imminent. But this two-letter word can be overused and confining.

When my children were young, I wanted to encourage them to be brave enough to engage the world around them. Accordingly, I usually tried things other than "no" to stop innocent offending behaviors (like feeding the dog chocolate or running *up* the down-slide). The word "no" by itself definitely would have stopped my children in their tracks, but it also would have stifled their spirit of exploration and conquest: "What would happen if I did *this*?" I was looking for the impact of a "no" without discouraging discovery. In addition, I wanted to teach my children to develop the ability to foresee the consequences of their actions.

How many ways can a parent say "no"? As a young mother, I sought an answer to that question. And my research is still ongoing. In fact, even though my children are now up and out, I continue the habit pattern I started way back when. The word "no" often gets stuck in my throat. And the pause it creates stimulates my search for better solutions.

My inspiration for exploring various and sundry substitutes for "no" was the fact that the word was ubiquitous. As I went about my busy life, I was overwhelmed by this one little word. "No" besieged me. It followed me everywhere. In public places, my head was spinning. To the right—"No, you can't have that candy." To the left—"No, put that magazine down." Behind me—"No, don't touch that display." In front of me—"No, stop bothering your sister." Sometimes the "no" was accompanied by a slap of the hand. Other times by a threat (I *won't* buy you that toy unless you stop.) Still, other times by bribery (I *will* buy you an ice cream cone if you stop.) Many of the parents I observed felt one "no" wasn't enough, so they fired multiple repetitions, machine-gun style—"No, no, no, no, no." If I, a passerby, felt assaulted by these limitations, imagine how the children who were receiving the messages felt.

So I came up with a plan I could live with: 1) to *teach* (not demand) my children to behave, 2) to encourage them to grow, develop, and challenge themselves, and 3) to limit the number of negative messages that communicated all of the things they *could not* do. I did not want my children to absorb *only* denial and refusal. And I did not want to build fences that would limit their creativity, enthusiasm, and drive (like the child who delights in coloring outside of the lines being forced with a "no" to stay inside of the lines). I wanted my kids' world to be a vast frontier of experimenting, building, and exploring. I wanted them to wonder at the complexity and beauty around them and to be brave enough to give things a try. But at the same time, the burden was clearly on me to stop offending behaviors that would have harmed them or aggravated the people around them.

How did I support my dreams for my children without creating mischievous monsters who didn't respect limits? How did I find the balance between innocent discovery and malicious mischief? How did I teach my children that a trip to the grocery was not a free-for-all, but an opportunity to enthuse about a bright and shiny color, to gush about an intriguing cereal box, or to gently reach out and touch a fuzzy something?

Over time my modus operandi ripened into this: I restrained my children's behavior when necessary, but did so in a way that did not shut them down, disparage them, or inhibit them. In other words, I didn't use the word "no" to create a world that was filled with things they *could not* do. (Please note, if safety was an issue, like a child running into the street, I did not hesitate to vocalize a loud and resounding "no!"). At the same time, I encouraged my children to experience and feel wonder at the world around them. In our family, the two opposing sides of this formula, restraint and encouragement, equaled success.

This theory may sound good on paper, as so many theories do. But how was I going to implement it? Self-discipline and quick thinking were key elements. The self-discipline part was to stop the mindless "no" that habitually tried to push its way up and out of my throat. The quick-thinking element was to flip through my Rolodex of alternatives and come up with a speedy surrogate solution.

First, let me give you a "no" example I witnessed with someone else's child. My family and another family had been invited to a friend's house for dinner. When we entered our friend's home, the smell of garlic and oregano permeated the air. The house was clean and beautifully decorated in anticipation of our visit. Displayed on the coffee table were an array of appetizers—crackers and cheese, stuffed mushrooms, flavored almonds. They were placed right next to Aunt Bertha's crystal vase, the one she delicately wrapped and transported across oceans until it acquired a new home in the United States.

The eyes of the other family's two-year-old son engaged and locked on that vase. As the light from a nearby lamp traveled through it, a myriad of colors paraded around the room. He focused. He could not see anything else. His mother noticed. She verbalized an order (without an explanation), "No, no, no! Don't touch!" A reprieve. The child disengaged his eyes. The mother felt she had done her job and sighed with relief. The vase was safe—for now.

We continued talking and laughing, and enjoying the hors d'oeuvres. But that two-year-old's mind was full of challenge and marvel at the magnificence of the vase. The child's mother took a sip from her wine glass. As her head tilted slowly back, her two-year-old took advantage of her diversion. He struck. Within the blink of an eye, it was over. The vase was scattered in a million glittery pieces on the hosts' polished hardwood floor. Everyone was aghast. The two-year old was reprimanded in a loud and pleading voice, "I *told* you not to touch that." The apologies erupted in a volcanic flow. But the damage was done. The hosts felt upset. The mother felt guilty. And the son felt repressed and humiliated—all because he marveled at the colors that sparkled from a beautiful crystal vase.

If we were to replay that scenario on my terms, it would go something like this: I am enjoying an evening with friends. As I am tasting and talking and listening, I notice my two-year-old's vision locking on Aunt Bertha's vase. I pause in my conversation. I get off the couch and relax on the floor next to my son. His expression communicates awe at the rainbow of colors splashed around the room. His hand instinctively reaches out to explore the phenomenon more intimately. My hand tenderly connects with his, before he reaches the vase. We share a private moment of sensory delight as I acknowledge the vase's beauty and splendor. He is focused on the vase and enriched by my words. In one sentence, I describe the vase's delicacy and explain what could happen if it were bumped or knocked over—a million glittery pieces. Then I wait for him to decide. He returns his outstretched hand to his lap. He chooses to preserve the beautiful vase and to consume it with eyes only. He remains filled with wonder; our hosts continue to lavish us with delectable treats and tales; and I am delighted at having shared a precious moment with my son. Everyone wins. I did not assume he had mischievous intent. Instead, I presumed he was enchanted. And all it took was a moment to explain what the consequences of a rash action could be.

I know what you are thinking. You don't have time to write a novel every time your child extends beyond his borders. And I agree. But most of these messages to my children were shared in seconds. And if one of the kids caught me by surprise, a quick "no" now was followed by an explanation later. My kids were thirsty to know *why*, and, when possible, I felt they deserved to quench that craving.

If Child A was pulling Child B's hair and causing a loud fuss in the back seat of the car, I had some choices. I could have shouted a knee-jerk "no." Instead, I tried a simple explanation. Here are some things I could have done: Describe how Child B felt when her hair was being pulled, the painful sensation of skin stretching beyond its tender limits. *Or* tell the kids how the fuss they were making made me, the driver, feel—distracted and upset. *Or* explain the safety issues associated with crashes and smashes. *Or* portray what life would be like without the family car (because our mechanic had to keep it for two weeks to make it whole again). In seconds, I would have made my case. Then I would have paused and let them absorb it. I would have given my kids a chance to make the decision to stop the yanking and the commotion. If they did, great. If they didn't, I would have changed gears, pulled the car over to the side of the road, and refused to travel another inch until I got what I needed—a quiet and peaceful automobile.

By not overusing "no," I helped my children learn that they *and the people around them* were affected by their choices. I helped them see that they had a hand in creating a happy environment. And I helped them foresee consequences to future actions.

My children have learned these lessons well. As a result, they have become planners—at work, at school, and at play. If they are arranging a trip, they look ahead. They don't want the "vase to drop." They are not fearful or paranoid—they simply are well prepared. They anticipate that they should pull back here and push forward there. The end result is a smoother, calmer ride for them and everyone else concerned.

My children thrived when they were given the opportunity to wonder, explore, and try new things. They pondered and appreciated the many marvels around them. They extended themselves and took some chances. But while they were at it, they learned that there are consequences to every choice. By having a mom who was willing to take a moment to teach them the value of thinking ahead, my children learned to safeguard their environment, explore their world, and participate in it with unabated enthusiasm.

OVERUSING "NO"
(TO YOUNG ADULTS)

YOU DON'T HAVE TO SAY
NO; YOU CAN ALWAYS
TAKE THE MATTER UNDER
ADVISEMENT.

After I wrote the previous chapter, "Overusing *No* (to Little Ones)," I e-mailed it to my children (as I do all of my chapters). They read about my attempts to stop a misbehavior without shrinking a child's world with "no, no, no." I received an immediate reaction from my philosophical daughter. She acknowledged that my thoughts (ceasing an action without constricting the drive to explore) were valuable, but she also thought the title "Overusing *No* "applied equally well to teenagers and young adults.

She said, "As we grew older, you let us discuss things with you. You never gave us a blanket 'no' without opening the subject up for dialogue or giving a reason why."

Then she added something that is imperative for all parents to understand: "I've seen dozens of parents say 'no' and then end the conversation with 'because I said so.' The result was that the kids didn't respond. The blanket 'no' just made them rebel instead of listen and learn. It made them angry at their parents and made them feel misunderstood and unheard."

My daughter continued with what she appreciated about her upbringing: "If I wanted to do something you weren't comfortable with, like making a seven-hour drive home from my college town by myself, you didn't act as if your word was law. You let me barter, compromise, and argue my case. The end result might have been that I chose the following weekend to come home so that I could drive with a friend; *or* that I spent the night at my brother's house, a halfway point, and made the trip in two days instead of one; *or* that I restricted my driving to daylight hours. But the real impact was that the process made me feel like a partner in my upbringing. It encouraged me to argue for what I believe in, and it honed my discussion skills. It also triggered me to listen to and respect your argument instead of automatically rebelling."

Boy, did it hone her discussion skills. In fact, it's pretty hard for me to keep up with her anymore. Most of the time she makes too much sense. Through years of negotiation, she learned that her parents responded to logic and common sense. It became her burden to sift through a myriad of emotions (like fear that something would go wrong with her car or helplessness if something did go wrong) and find a logical path to an end point that could be accepted by both parties. And her brothers have become equally adept.

I am *not* saying that you should never say "no." Because when it comes to health and safety, it is necessary to stop all discussion and take immediate action—and that action may be a big, resounding "no."

If your teenager wants to spend the weekend at a friend's house with no parental supervision, the first thing that should come out of your mouth is a big, loud "no." If your teenager wants to bend the law by driving a friend someplace when the rules clearly state that new licensees must drive alone for the first six months, a "no" is perfectly appropriate. You may want to follow your "no" with a short discussion of why these things are not allowed, but your initial response should be clear. And it should be stated in a way that communicates that this is not negotiable.

Kids want to know why. They have always wanted to know why. And that is an enviable quality. When they are little they want to understand why they have to take a bath every day. And when they are older, they want to understand why they can't stay up until midnight on school nights. I think it is important for parents to be in the habit of explaining these things. Why? The conversations encourage children to continue to be curious. The knowledge they gain prepares them for upcoming challenges. The concepts they are introduced to teach them important lessons about potential outcomes and consequences. And the discussions (and sometimes negotiations) they engage in reduce resentment—which increases harmony in the home.

That doesn't mean that my children got everything they wanted. But it does mean that they felt like part of the process. They felt that they had given input and that they had been listened to. And once in a while, after they contributed a good dose of logic and common sense, they discovered that they had the power and technique to make some changes.

If our job as parents is to prepare our children for a successful adulthood, then it is imperative that we teach them real-life survival skills. If something is unfair in the classroom, it falls upon us to teach them how to deal with the situation. If something is unfair in the home environment, it is our job to instruct them how to think their way through it. Explanation, conversation, and negotiation are key elements. A blanket "no" in non-threatening situations leaves little room for challenge and growth.

As my daughter mentioned, it is vital that we teach our young people how to barter, compromise, and argue (logically and respectfully, of course). These skills are not only useful, they are critical in an academic setting, in the employment arena, and within a family structure.

I tried to train my children to understand that they were not always going to get everything they wanted, but maybe, with the right skills, they could meet the other party halfway. As they learned to present a solid case for attending a concert in a distant city, for example, I let them know that I also had a valid point of view and they needed to listen to it, consider it, and process it. It was understood that the final word was mine. But could we reach a compromise? Would they agree to have me, their dad, or another parent accompany them? Or would the discussion be postponed until they were older and wiser?

Everyone's opinions were important in our family. But if I had holes in my argument (which I often had), I wanted my children to be skilled at finding them and negotiating their way through them. When they learned to do this capably (and unemotionally), the result was respect—the respect my children received *from* their parents and the respect my children felt *toward* their parents, who took the time to listen and reason with them. Of course, arguments did not have to be free of emotion. Emotions are okay. But arguments could not be based solely on emotion. The kids learned that a passionate position delivered with structure and good sense can be very effective.

Throughout this process, my children developed *self-respect*. Self-respect was the by-product of learning to skillfully confront issues in their teenage world. The end may or may not have gone their way, but the means made them feel successful every time.

From the time my children were little, they wanted to grow up. They pushed themselves to vocalize a new word, take another step, and demonstrate independence in a variety of ways. I wanted to give them the skills that, when used appropriately, would make them feel that they were valuable members of the family and that they were "growing up." This gift of discussion and negotiation, instead of reactive refusals, helped them avoid defiant acts designed to prove that they were, indeed, "grown up."

Adults who stand up for what they believe in are admired by the rest of us. How do these people—who openly display integrity, common sense, and logic—develop excellent communication skills, inspire us to listen, and motivate us to think? Can a child who is continually told, "No, you can't do this," and "No, you can't do that," develop into a highly regarded adult who takes stands? I am sure it can be done and has been done, but I believe the undertaking would involve extra effort and struggle. Wouldn't it be easier for children to cultivate these enviable skills if we taught them how they can respectfully and competently affect the world around them?

Children have lessons to teach us and points of view to share. My children have enlightened me and my husband in ways we never believed possible. They have each developed a moral code that is true to themself. I can influence their code, and they can influence mine. But if any one of us is going to try to persuade the other, we had better approach the situation with the proper skills in hand. We had better demonstrate a clear thought process, rationality, judgment, and courage, because holes in the fabric of an argument will be identified and responded to politely—but without hesitation.

I now see that articulation, negotiation, and compromise— and the self-respect these things produced—were essential to my children building indispensable, real-world skills. I encourage all parents to prepare their children for an adulthood that enables them to exercise some authority. Instead of stunting a child's process with a constant barrage of "no, no, no," I favor the promotion of logic, discussion, and concession when appropriate. I wanted my children to feel that they *do* have the power to convince others (including their parental authority figures) and that they *can* make a difference if they develop the courage to stand up for what they believe in. Without that knowledge, they could too easily have developed into unmotivated adults who had learned not even to try.

PRAISE

Have you ever walked into a room and heard people whispering praise about someone who is in the vicinity but just out of earshot? The whisperers don't want the subject to hear them. They take pains to keep their voices low. Does hearing praise damage the psyche of the receiver? Does it contribute to the development of ego-driven and narcissistic personalities?

As a young mom, I asked myself how I could raise children who were proud and confident, but not arrogant. I wondered, "If I do manage to raise self-assured children, how do I put a cap on it? How do I keep them from becoming big-headed, overconfident teenagers and adults?" I wanted my children to develop personalities that would be welcomed socially and professionally by others (peers, teachers, professors, coworkers, employers, and friends), but could I raise them to become capable, confident, *and* understated?

I came up with a plan to deal with these issues, and it ended up working very well. I raised three confident yet modest children. Because of that success, I feel secure in saying that I have a one-word answer to the above questions—praise. But praise needs to be given thoughtfully and meaningfully—not vacantly and superficially.

When my children were young, I did not want to instill a sense of "I am wonderful" in them if they hadn't earned it. I wanted the praise I bestowed to be genuine. When one of my children did something that deserved admiration, I noticed it and rewarded it at an age-appropriate level—not with whispers to an uninterested passerby, but directly to the child himself. In this way, through hundreds of character-building episodes, I was able to help my children mold their behavior, develop faith in their abilities, and cultivate unassuming natures.

My praise strategy began when my children were young, mere toddlers, and openly accepting of parental ideas. (When my kids became teenagers, they seemed less dependent on parental input and more involved with measuring their character against that of their peers.) The first step I took was to activate my maternal eagle-eyes. I turned them on and tuned them in whenever I was with my children. I watched and noticed everything. If my child picked up a toy and shared it with a playmate, I spotted it—just like a predator spots its prey. Then I pounced and announced, "You shared your toy with so-and-so. That was generous of you. You are a kind person." Finished! I never overdid it with oozing acclaim. The praise I gave was succinct, deserved, and believable. It was simple and factual: You did *this*. That demonstrated *this* quality. Therefore, you possess *this* attribute. One, two, three. In mere seconds it was done.

My chapter on fear discusses the value of eye contact, physical touch, and voice intonation when building a parent-child relationship. Well, all three elements were involved in my praise strategy as well, but they were moving in the opposite direction. My fear chapter describes the piercing eye contact, firm physical touch, and commanding voice intonation I used when establishing my role as an authority figure. Giving praise involved *relaxed* eye contact, *gentle* physical touch, and *soothing* voice intonation. As I uttered words of praise to my children—who had no idea that what they had done was significant—my eyes *calmly* gazed into theirs, hoping to propel my message directly into their developing identities. My look was accompanied by a *melodious* voice, meant to evoke comfort and trust. And my tone was reinforced by a *sweet* touch—of a dimpled arm, a chubby cheek, or a handful of tangled hair.

At the end of my routine, my children always enjoyed my concluding words, the ones that made them sit a little taller and smile a little wider: "I am proud of you." The realization that their parents were proud of them was important to my children. They delighted in the knowledge that their parents approved of and admired them. As a result, they worked hard to maintain that standing.

To this day, my children call me often to share their adventures and accomplishments. When they hear the appreciation in my voice, I believe they travel back in time and wrap themselves, once again, in the warmth of many past childhood praises. Parental pride that was deserved and sincere helped transform my tentative children—who were struggling to establish distinctiveness and a sense of self—into confident, creative, and generous souls.

As my praise system played itself out over time, it helped my children develop a variety of characteristics. Generosity—sharing a toy—was easy. When my children received their "You-are-a-kind-person" praise after sharing a toy or a cookie or a turn on the swing, they soon started searching for other things to share so that they could, once more, enjoy Mom's recognition of their actions. After hearing a particular praise repeated enough times, they began to perceive that sharing a toy or a turn was important not simply for Mom's approval but because it was the right thing to do. Sharing helped the world flow a little more harmoniously. After all, Mom and Dad were so pleased with them when they did it.

After repeated praise taught my kids what their parents approved of and what they didn't, the kids proceeded on autopilot. They began sharing, caring, and creating without depending on their parents' reaction. Generosity with toys and taking turns became part of their character. They no longer shared merely for a reward. They shared because they had learned that it was the right thing to do.

This praise system worked equally well for other qualities. If one of my children finished a difficult homework assignment— like a multi-page written report—I noticed his hard work. And that child heard from me. I told him that I thought he was capable and talented: "You worked hard, and this report is well done. I am impressed by your writing and imagination. I am proud of you."

And it worked for "smart," too. The proof lies with my middle son, who, while very bright, grappled with a learning disability. I wanted so much for him to realize that even though he struggled, he was intelligent and he could succeed academically. If he could absorb that thought, then I could send him into a post-high school world with the confidence and skills he needed to contribute positively in his unique way.

For this child, praise was an important part of a *bigger* program. First, my husband and I took a practical approach that involved teaching our son how to break things down into small, workable parts. Next, we used praise for things that were done well. Finally, we helped him understand that his particular challenge was going to help him develop into a person who can work harder and understand deeper than many of his peers— and that is the exact result he got.

I was touched when this grown son, who had been grappling with a particular obstacle in his adult educational/professional life, told me, "Mom, I know I'm smart." To this day, he doesn't know that I had tears in my eyes when I heard him casually utter those words. I felt I had contributed to his sense of self. He had assimilated what we were trying to teach him. And now his future has no limits.

In summary, my method of helping instill a quiet confidence into my children's character and an honest ability to handle life's upcoming challenges looked like this: 1) I noticed what they did, and I took the time to stop whatever I was doing to let them know I noticed; 2) I expressed my delight at the quality I felt they displayed ("You are smart. You are creative. You are generous. You are a problem solver. You are a leader. You are kind. You are brave."); 3) I used several sensory pathways to reinforce my praise message (friendly eye contact, an I-love-you voice, and playful physical touch); and 4) I delivered these simple words: "I am proud of you."

Again, the praise I delivered was deserved and genuinely given. If my children didn't believe me or, even worse, if they *did* believe me based on artificial evidence, I could have contributed to little monsters in the making, children with large egos based on empty skills and attributes. But the praise I gave was valid, and the children did believe it. By the time my kids were teenagers, they no longer depended on my praise. They still enjoyed it, but they were much more capable of weighing their character against the behavior and decisions of others in their age group. They began to do the right things not for a reward, but because, through repetition, they had absorbed a sense of right and wrong.

My children have developed into confident yet humble, capable yet kind young adults. I credit praise, as my husband and I used it, as a crucial component of my children's character-building process. My kids are good people today because they believed they were good people when they were younger. They live their lives today consistent with the decisions they made about themselves when they were younger.

I have seen parents praise their kids to others but silence themselves when their children approached. These parents are afraid that their praise will go to their children's heads. But that's exactly what I wanted to happen. I wanted my praise to go to my children's heads. I wanted them to believe my praise and use it to make decisions about themselves that would build their character and integrity and support them in the complicated years ahead.

Going back to my original question—does hearing praise damage the psyche of the receiver—I can comfortably answer yes and no. Yes, praise that is given when no praise has been earned can create a false sense of self that can tumble like a house of cards when it is challenged. And no, praise that is given sincerely after it has been earned cannot do damage. To the contrary, it can build a firm foundation upon which a child can develop into a confident and capable adult who can distinguish between appropriate and inappropriate behavior.

People who have a false sense of confidence may easily be able to attract associates and positions through charisma and braggadocio. But they can just as easily disappoint everyone around them when their talk proves to be nothing more than empty words. A subtly confident young person, on the other hand, will amaze people over time as their strengths and abilities are revealed one little surprise at a time—just like a time-released capsule. Our esteem for these types of people continues to grow far into the future.

 PUNISHMENT

THE PARENT WHO DOES
NOT PUNISH CANNOT
PERSUADE.

I remember times I punished my children—many times. But my memory is not of sullen expressions, angry voices, slamming doors, or high-pitched yells. Instead, it is often of negotiation, creativity, cooperation— and even laughter.

How could that be? Punishment is supposed to be a time when children feel the wrath of their parents and the consequences of their actions. But punishment can also be a time for children to experience growth, education, and clarity. It can be a time for building character and developing honor.

When my kids were small, I made up my mind that punishment, while inevitable, would be meaningful. I did not want to waste this fertile ground on knee-jerk time-outs and groundings (although there are times that these tools are useful). My job as a young parent was to eventually send *good* people out into the world. So I wanted to take advantage of every opportunity I had to develop decency in my children. It's easy to send a child to his or her room. And it has its advantages: a little peace and quiet for the parents (while the errant child is entertaining himself with the TV, DVD, CD player, X-Box, and computer that adorn his room), and a return to harmony in the household. But are there other options that would encourage reflection, concession, and evolution?

I tried to remain flexible with regard to punishment. I understood that I needed to handle a child who purposely hurt someone else more harshly than a child who carelessly experimented with clay in a toilet that soon protested and shut itself down. And I knew that health and safety episodes, like recklessly running into a street, needed to be handled quickly and authoritatively. But I felt that the average, day-to-day issues should be tailored to each unique incident. Sometimes I sent my kids to their rooms—so that I would have time to think and respond meaningfully. Other times I asserted myself as a dictator. But *most* of the time, my children and I worked on punishment together in a cooperative spirit.

Even though I don't have a clear recollection of one of my daughter's offending behaviors, I do have a vivid memory of the punishment *process*. What comes to mind is that she did something—thoughtlessly and wantonly—that resulted in damage to something that was precious to another family member. After my daughter had done her deed, I could read the anxiety on her face. I felt her tension as she stood frozen before me.

I said to myself, "Intuition, please kick in. What can I say to her that will give her the consequences she needs to experience and the lessons she needs to learn about respecting the belongings of others, the space of others, and the attachments we all make to certain items?"

I decided to involve my daughter in a punishment process that involved negotiation and reparation. Right now you are probably shaking your heads thinking, "Negotiation? Don't children need to learn that they can't weasel out of impending consequences?" The reason I added a give-and-take exchange is because the process empowers the negotiators. I wanted my children to feel their consequence, but not at the expense of feeling powerless in front of me or anyone else. I wanted to teach them when they were young that they had *some* influence on me with regard to punishment and that that influence one day would empower them to solve other more adult problems on their own. I hoped other lessons could be taught, as well: taking responsibility for one's actions, self-governance, and treating other's (and their things) with respect.

It always surprised me—every single time—that when I involved my children in an inevitable and imminent punishment, that they were harder on themselves than I ever would have been. And I told them so. But they always insisted that their way, although stricter or requiring an extra investment of time and energy, was a better balance for the offense.

So I asked my daughter this question: "What are we going to do about this?" And then the negotiations began.

Number 1, the broken fragments had to be bandaged or disposed of. We both agreed on that. So far so good.

Number 2, a lesson about respect for the property of others had to be learned. This was a good time to bring out my library of ethics books. Ah, here we go. Three short chapters that cover topics related to the value of personal possessions, appreciating what does not belong to you, and honoring others.

I authoritatively said, "Read these three chapters and report to me what you learned. We will discuss it." Some grumbling on her part.

"One chapter," she snapped. She inclined her body forward, focused her eyes on mine, and waited for my response.

"Two chapters," I countered, "and you get to choose which two."

Agreed!

At this point you might be thinking that using ethics books for punishment would teach my kids to disdain ethics. I disagree. Ethics conversations worked in our home because I spent time with my children discussing the principles. My kids enjoyed the one-on-one sessions they shared with me as we tossed around concepts and came to conclusions. These were lively, stimulating conversations. And afterwards, we all felt elevated and enlivened.

Now to Number 3, the fun part. I said, "You must replace what was lost with something equally beautiful." Quiet contemplation on her part. I could see the gears turning.

"Got it," she bubbles. "But I can't tell you what it is, and you can't see it until I am done."

"Agreed," I added. A look of pure satisfaction decorated her face.

Number 4, physical effort. I proposed, "You must write something short, one page, about what happened here today and what you learned, and you have to hand it to me by the end of the day."

"Huhm," she mumbled. I could tell that the last thing she wanted to do was write a report about the episode. She took a few moments to think and then countered.

"How about I write a report, but I get to choose the topic?"

Now it was my turn to mumble, "Huhm."

At that point I felt that a little flexibility on my part was going to make a big difference in the tone of our relationship for the rest of the day. I wanted to choose my battles wisely.

"Okay," I responded. "You've got a deal."

Handshakes. A synchronized nodding of heads. We both felt that we had negotiated a good deal. I was able to enforce some meaningful consequences. She was able to atone for her irresponsibility with a little time and effort.

What would have happened if I had not negotiated a deal? My daughter probably would have taken her sad, mad emotions into her room and contemplated how unfair life was and how best to rebel against it.

Because we negotiated, we both ended up feeling satisfied with the result. My daughter had input and expressed her ideas. She felt she had won a battle (which can be very empowering when you are up against an authority figure). And we both felt we had contributed to the cease-fire that ended the war.

So instead of sending my daughter to her room, I fashioned a multilayered consequence that was designed for this particular episode. Here's how it ended up.

Number 1, the mess was cleaned up. Definitely to my benefit.

Number 2, two short chapters of life lessons were read willingly from an author of my choice—and discussed. To both of our benefits.

Number 3, a creative collage! My daughter's idea to replace what was missing was a beautiful one. She spent time perusing photograph albums—those telling reminiscences of family events: trips to Yosemite, horseback rides, birthday parties, Halloween costumes, Thanksgiving meals, graduations, weddings, bar mitzvahs, friends, cousins, beach outings, and more. For her project she chose squares of camera color that reflected our past, making sure everyone was represented equally.

During the day, I had no idea that she was working on a collage. All I heard was, "Mom, do we have a cork board?" and "Mom, do we have more push pins?"

I remember thinking, "What in the world is she doing over there?"

Then she presented it—an original art piece. Fragments of our family's history were placed lovingly on a board that was to hang in the victimized room. I will never forget the look of pride on her face as we hung her masterpiece on the wall. It was a lovely way to make amends for past losses. She was happy—and so was I.

Number 4, the report. I knew my daughter had a quirky sense of humor, something she must have picked up from the boys. So I knew I couldn't predict the subject of her thesis. But I certainly did hear her enthusiasm and wonderment as she was creating it.

I heard her exclaim, "I didn't know that. Wow!"

The Internet was working hard to answer her probing

questions. She went from one site to another until she found what she was looking for.

"Okay, Mom. Here it is."

Her report was not handed to me on a flimsy, worn, disregarded piece of paper. Oh, no. The multipage report was bestowed tenderly and considerately in a clear plastic cover, inscribed with a generous title, and decorated with a descriptive piece of art.

"TOOTHPASTE," I read. I laughed aloud, and she was delighted by my reaction. We learned more about toothpaste that day—its history and evolution—than we ever thought possible. We had such a good time together as she was being punished.

At this point you might be asking yourselves how a report on toothpaste could teach my daughter a lesson. How does toothpaste relate to the offense? In this particular situation, it didn't. But I was open to her topic negotiation because her deed did not involve a mean spirit or cause harm to another human being. She was touching something she shouldn't have touched, something that belonged to someone else. And she was careless with the item. What was important to me was that she willingly engaged in the punishment exercise, and that she felt empowered to help define the parameters. If she had cruelly hurt another person, I am sure I would have been stricter in my approach.

Throughout this process, my daughter learned about consequences to actions. Instead of spending the day banished in her room, she exerted time and effort to repair what she had damaged. But she also learned about respecting others, making amends, and the joy of a job well done—as well as an awful lot about the evolution of toothpaste.

The method of negotiation and free choice within boundaries that we implemented that day helped my daughter feel pride in her accomplishments (her collage and report). She was able to take on her punishment *without anger or rebellion*. She read from a book I chose because she agreed to do it, not because she was forced to. She learned her lessons well that day. After all, she helped fashion them.

RELIGION

IF WE COULD FIRST KNOW
WHERE WE ARE, AND
WHITHER WE ARE
TENDING, WE COULD
BETTER JUDGE WHAT TO
DO, AND HOW TO DO IT.
—ABRAHAM LINCOLN

Who am I? Where do I fit in? What does it all mean?

These are questions my children started asking way back when and have continued to ask throughout their lifetimes. I felt it was healthy for my children to probe the meaning of life deeply. It meant that they were yearning to give sense and significance to human existence. People around the world—those living in the smallest, most secluded villages and those residing in the biggest, brightest urban centers—have always asked the same searching questions. I wanted to help my children seek their own personal answers. I sensed that the spiritual journey they were about to take would become a springboard of values from which they would make many future decisions.

Do I introduce my children to organized religion, to a code of ethics, or do I not? Do I force them to go to weekly services, or not? Do I send them to a religious youth group, or not? Do I incorporate God-based (Goddess-based, Universe-based, Spirit-based, Humanist-based, Energy-based, or whatever-based you want to call it) rituals into my family's daily life, or not? Do I let my children investigate religion themselves and decide for themselves, or not? These are questions many parents grapple with.

The particular religion my husband and I associate with has a peoplehood component that is attractive to me. You can be born into Judaism or be converted into it. Either way, you are part of the Jewish people, and you are as responsible for fellow Jews in Ethiopia as you are to members of your local synagogue. Behavior is stressed over belief. The faith part is pretty much up to you—yes, I believe; no, I don't believe; I believe but I am angry; I don't believe but I practice certain rituals; I kind of believe but I have a Buddhist bent—whatever angle you choose to take. What is most important in Judaism is that you struggle with the philosophical and theological ideas and that you behave ethically.

I care how people conduct themselves. Your behavior (honesty in the workplace, kindness to those less fortunate, and generosity to those in need) affects me—and everyone else, for that matter. So I supported presenting a moral code of guidance to my children. I chose to introduce that code through one religion—Judaism. Other parents to whom these issues are important choose religions that resonate with them. And still others choose a secular lifestyle that embodies a strong moral code.

I have heard some parents say that they are not offering any type of religious training to their children because they don't want to force such a personal decision. They think that one day inspiration will fall from above and—poof—their children will choose to be this religion or that. I believe it is difficult for teenagers and young adults to become inspired to conduct themselves morally and ethically in a complicated world. And that challenge is compounded when they have no awareness of what a code of conduct could mean in their lives, or of the tools available to help them make wise decisions.

I have heard other parents say they are offering multiple religions so their children can make up their own minds when they get older. These parents believe in offering a buffet of choices, all equally valid. They open brightly wrapped gifts in the shadow of a Christmas tree while a Chanukah menorah shines brightly in the window. They decorate lavender-and-gold Easter eggs as they munch on flat, dry Passover matzoh. These parents think that variety and options are key to future moral stability. But I think it would be very hard for young adults to comprehend the value of a solid and comprehensive moral structure, and to use it when they feel conflicted, if there are too many options to choose from. Each one would seem diluted by the existence of the others.

(I have to add a qualifier here. Teaching religion is different from celebrating religion—with trees and eggs and candles and festive foods. The meaning and values gleaned from the study and discussion of one religion, many religions, or irreligious ideas can all contribute to a sturdy code of behavioral conduct.)

Am I saying to parents who offer many religions to their children that less knowledge (one religion) is more? Do I think that a child who is offered one religion in the home will behave better than a child who is raised in a you'll-make-up-your-mind-when-you're-ready home? And do I think that secular families believe a code of behavior is unimportant? Of course not. I value the study of comparative religion and the incorporation of behavioral standards into homes without a focused religious base. But after raising three children and observing their thought processes, I believe their developing minds saw things more clearly in black-and-white than they did in shades of gray. In other words, it was more effective for me to say to my elementary-school-age children, "Do this because. . . and don't do this because . . . ." rather than confuse them with conflicting theological concepts—or no concepts at all.

I believe my children benefited from the introduction of one consistent religious moral code. As they matured and their minds became capable of handling more complex ideas, they were free to test that religion. They could rebel against it, question it, reject it, or accept it. But whatever path they took, the underlying principles they were offered supported them and guided them in the years ahead.

Like most other people, my husband and I decided to celebrate the culture, tradition, and moral guidelines of the one religion we were most versed in and comfortable with, the one we were born into. We never attempted to make a statement that our religious beliefs were better than any other, but we did say that our religious beliefs made the most sense to us—and a practicing Catholic's religion made the most sense to him, and a practicing Protestant's religion made the most sense to her. We liked the "this-world focus" of Judaism, and we accepted it exclusively as our base of operation. We raised our children in the faith we were born into, and we hoped that this immersion would enable our children to understand the significant role religion can play in one's life. By offering one religion in the home, we trusted that our adult children would be able to make their personal religious choices based on something solid underneath their feet.

To us, offering one religion meant living those religious beliefs. It meant raising our children a certain way (religious school, bar and bat mitzvahs, holidays, discussions, codes of behavior, et cetera). But what if our grown children found the structure to be unstable, convoluted, or contradictory? What if they felt limited? Once they began living their adult lives, *they received no pressure from us*. We honored them as adults who had developed a foundation from which they could make the right decision *for them*. They could either continue on the path we had followed as a family, or alter the path to one that satisfied their unique inner quest.

My husband and I consistently presented the Jewish code we lived by. We searched for depth, joy, and meaning in everyday actions. We contemplated, questioned, and discussed, as I think it is human nature to do. And then, when the kids became of age, we stepped back and observed how the children were going to use the the information they had accumulated.

The results have been a mixed bag. So far, one of my children feels deeply about having one religion, Judaism, in his home. One of my children, who has been an ardent student of comparative religion, is an atheist. And one of my children is inspired by a spiritual approach that lacks religious dogma. The important thing for me, their mom, to remember is that these very personal choices *were not mine to make*. My children became good adults. They never considered stealing something from a workplace, cheating someone for profit, or taking advantage of someone else for gain. Why? Because based on everything they had learned at home, they knew that these acts were wrong. No matter what their final religious decisions are, my children are living by a strong code of ethics. I accept their adult choices. My job is done.

When my children were young, I committed myself to monitoring their behavior and teaching them to be ethical and honorable people. There are various ways to do that, both religious and secular. (I realize that removing religion does not necessarily mean abandoning a standard of justice and morality; productive family discussions can help a child become a better person.) But my husband and I chose to raise our children with the beauty and richness of one religion that could act as a launching pad to our children's inevitable search for the answers to big questions. A connection to something bigger or a dedication to a standard of behavior must be felt deeply in the heart and in the mind in order to be put into practice. How can children determine what the right thing is if they have not been introduced to any guidelines (or too many guidelines)? Do they merely make decisions based on what *feels* right to them at the moment?

Many people of the Jewish persuasion would strongly disagree with my acceptance of my children's adult choices. They believe in a Jewish bloodline. I love my Judaism, but for the world's sake, I believe in character, integrity, and honor first—however that is developed. The path people take to achieve goodness is less important to me than the fact that they have embraced the challenge and taken steps to move forward. The love of bloodlines has caused much heartache in the world. If the people who committed atrocities in the name of blood were nurtured by their parents, instead, to embrace values of goodness, justice, ethics, and respect, perhaps millions of lives could have been saved.

I am not ignoring genes here. My guess is that if we studied goodness, we would find that a portion of it can be attributed to "good" genes. Some people who have been born into difficult or dangerous families have risen above the experience to become good adults. And other people who have been raised without religious backgrounds have developed into equally fine adults. But my proposition is that kids' minds respond well to a consistent right-and-wrong approach. So even though there was lots of questioning and discussion in our household, underneath it all was a strong support system sustained by principles, culture, ritual, and history. Good behavior was the ultimate goal, and having one stable religion was the tool my husband and I chose to reach it. Each of my children incorporated the lessons they learned uniquely, and each was touched in a positive way. To quote something my middle son recently said, "Judaism helped make me a better secularist."

I have learned so much from my children's spiritual quests and discoveries. In fact, I have now adopted a metaphysical bent to my Judaism, which was inspired—to my surprise—by my collision course with mystical Judaism, something I never even knew existed until a relatively short while ago. I have kept an open mind. I have continued to grow. My children have kept open minds. And they continue to develop. They know what questions to ask. They know the results they are looking for. They know what to compare their findings to. I hope I helped make this process more accessible to them by offering one stable religion throughout their childhood years.

RESPECT AND PRIVACY

THERE WAS NO RESPECT
FOR YOUTH WHEN I WAS
YOUNG, AND NOW I AM
OLD, THERE IS NO RESPECT
FOR AGE—I MISSED IT
COMING AND GOING.
—J.B. PRIESTLEY

Throughout my child-rearing years, I struggled with the idea of ownership—what belonged to my children and what did not. Did their possessions belong to me while they lived in my home? After all, they occupied a space that my husband and I worked very hard to provide for them. They didn't pay the mortgage that provided them a place to sleep. They didn't shop for the fruit roll-ups and the veggies and dip. They didn't shell out cash for clothes and shoes—shorts and sandals in the summertime, sweatshirts and tennis shoes in the wintertime. And they didn't pay for all of those movies—one blockbuster hit after another. Did they have the right to privacy and respect with regard to space, time, and possessions? Everything they supposedly "owned" or did was a result of their father and I either buying it or arranging it. Well, after years of pondering that question, here is my best answer: yes and no.

This answer may sound unsatisfactory at first blush, but this yes-and-no philosophy actually worked well for me. When my children were still small, I decided that, yes, they did have rights of ownership—of space (their rooms), of time (free time), and of things (diaries, journals, letters, et cetera)—*conditionally*. And the condition was this: as long as *things* were going well. And what were those *things*? School work, extracurricular activities, social life, interaction with family members, attitude, conduct— I'm sure you get the picture.

My condition for privacy was centered on character issues only—not mistakes or accidents or moods or childhood sluggishness. And any action taken by me was taken after I talked with my child and heard the other side of the story. If a teacher called to inform me of disruptive behavior or an anger problem in the classroom, my children knew they would likely suffer suspended or limited privacy rights. If one of them had come home from a party looking rumpled and "suspicious," again, suspended or limited privacy rights. If one of them had talked disrespectfully or used a colorful expletive to another family member or authority figure, suspended or limited privacy rights. If one of them had slipped money from my wallet or from the "cookie jar," suspended or limited privacy rights. If one of them had done anything that caused me to be suspicious of their motives and character, suspended or limited privacy rights.

And what would a loss of privacy have looked like? It would have looked like their mother had become gainfully employed as a hard working detective. It would have looked like snooping— with clear, immediate, and authoritative notice. In any of the above situations, I would have had no qualms about reading a diary or journal, listening to a private conversation, looking through drawers for who-knows-what, checking a room for hidden substances, asking a friend, talking to a teacher, checking e-mails—you name it. Since there might have been an innocent explanation for the behavior, I would have given the suspect some warning: "Because I am concerned about this or that, I am going to read your journal." Then, depending on their explanation, I would do it—or not.

And why would I not hesitate to become a sleuthhound and follow a fishy track wherever it took me? Easy! *For the safety, protection, and integrity of my children.* I would have done whatever it took to get them back on the safety track. And that means I would have been willing to withstand passionate and manipulative cries of "You don't trust me. That is confidential. That belongs to me. I have no privacy in this house. This is not fair. I'm a person, too!"

The purpose of the snooping would have been to discover the core problem—the one that was causing the troubling behavior. Was it rejection by a friend? Was it a frustrating learning situation? Was it pressure from someone to do something dangerous or malicious? Was it being treated unjustly at home? Once the origin was determined, a plan to resolve it could be made.

Afterward, the privilege of privacy and possession could be earned back. After all, I wanted my children to feel they had a measure of privacy and ownership. That belief taught them to take care of their possessions and to exert limited authority over their young lives. I didn't want my kids to think that nothing they "owned" was sacred. My children appreciated the privacy I gave them; they never took it for granted.

Do you want to know the funniest thing about this approach? I never had to use it—not once. My children understood that I had the last word in our home. They were welcome to give input, but the final decision was mine. They recognized that the respect I had for their space, time, and things was a privilege—not a right. They comprehended that their privacy was theirs to enjoy—as long as my suspicions were not aroused. They realized through experience that I had a sixth sense that could perceive the slightest questionable change in facial expressions. They learned the hard way that I knew when they were lying or hiding something.

Good kids are bad liars, and thank goodness for that. They simply are not skilled at telling tall tales. On the other hand, parents are *very* good at intuiting lies and other off-the-mark behavior. Parents can use this gift to guide their children toward healthier, more productive lives.

Remember, this FBI takeover of the family home was to kick in for character-related issues only (lying, stealing, cheating, dishonesty, hurting others, or committing illegal acts, to name a few). Therefore, nobody lost anything private or personal if a room was not cleaned, if hair was not combed, if an accident occurred, if food was sneaked into a bed at night, if books were read after lights out, if brother and sister had a fight, or if a child disagreed with a parent—respectfully.

My children were aware that their privileges were, indeed, privileges, and they cherished them. They knew how precious— and fragile—they were. They knew that the ticket to respect and privacy was good behavior. And good behavior was the option that each of them chose.

But occasionally a "fuzzy" area cropped up. An example is my daughter's high school yearbook. One activity my children always looked forward to was receiving their annual yearbook and getting their friends to sign it, each in their own inimitable style—misspellings and all. And it was an event I looked forward to as well. Reading the witty, charming anecdotes gave me insight as to how my children related to and were accepted by their peers. I could pick up clues that my children were welcomed or admired as friends, that they were thought to be talented or cute, or that they were appreciated and loved. Fun stuff.

One particular year, I sat down to look at my daughter's high school yearbook—to see her pictures, to feel pride in her involvements and accomplishments, and yes, to read her friends' entries. One writing stuck out in my mind, and I made a comment about it when my daughter returned home. Well, she was outraged. And I was shocked.

A lively discussion ensued. Her side: This was private. These were comments written for her eyes only, not to be digested by others. I had breached her privacy privilege *without cause*.

My side: I paid for the yearbook. And there was precedent.

I had always enjoyed reading all of the kids' yearbooks, and my family read my yearbooks way back when. In fact, my parents, siblings, and I used to peruse the yearbooks together—as a family activity. And we had so much fun doing it.

My daughter and I could not come to a compromise. It was one of those moments when you had to agree to disagree.

I didn't understand the need for secrecy in a yearbook. If you want to communicate something private, write a letter, for goodness sake. Don't express inner emotions on pages that are going to be passed around from person to person for days and years on end. According to her, I was allowed to look at the printed pages—no problem—but not the personal writings.

She didn't buy my argument that there would be no yearbook if I didn't pay for it, and that the process of reading it was so enjoyable and elucidating to me.

So we decided to poll the rest of the family. Her brothers agreed with her, of course—yearbook owners that they were. My husband felt I should have asked for her permission before I read personal writings directed to her. He's the wise one in the family. And that's how it ended—a reluctant resolution for me. I still struggled with the concept of yearbook privacy, but I did cooperate. As long as she gave me nothing to be suspicious about, I respected her wishes.

This yearbook experience was an eye opener for me. Times, indeed, had changed. Do you want to know what some typical entries were in my old yearbooks? "You're not very pretty, and your manners are few, but just remember, the mighty oak tree was once a nut like you." Or, "Some people write up, some people write down, but I'll be different and write all around" (written in a circle around the perimeter of the page)." Or the ever popular, "Roses are red, violets are pink. Now I'm wasting darn good ink." Did I ever care who read my yearbook entries? Absolutely not—because there was nothing personal written there.

In contrast, today's children tailor their written entries to each and every yearbook they inscribe. They pour out their feelings in their annual contributions. The writings are bright and they are humorous. They are also personal. Who would have known? Not this "roses-are-red-and-violets-are-blue" mom.

So this was the bottom line for my kids with regard to respect and privacy: With good behavior you earn respect and privacy—your diaries, letters, e-mails, and yearbooks (added reluctantly) are yours. With suspicious behavior, however, no stone will be left unturned—for your safety and protection. So safeguard your privileges, children. You are in total control here.

And this was the bottom line for my husband and me: Respect your children's space, time, and possessions. But when safety, protection, or character issues rise to the surface, do not hold back. A frontal attack may be in order. You may have to check computer e-mails, Internet usage, or personal phone lines. You may have to take locks off bedroom doors, ban friends from private spaces, or inspect diaries and journals.

It was not a bad lesson for my kids to learn that many things, even private things like diaries, were conditional, and that they did not deserve certain privileges merely because they breathed in and out every day. Many things, even private things like e-mail messages and phone conversations, had to be earned by good behavior. And because my children worked for these things, they appreciated them and chose to behave in a way that ensured they could keep them—from yearbook to yearbook to yearbook.

To this day, I don't know what was written on the pages of my children's journals, what words were spoken in their telephone conversations, and what thoughts were sent through cyberspace. My children enjoyed parental respect of their privacy. But they knew that my husband and I were ready to put on our detective hats at a moment's notice. My kids did whatever they could to ensure that we kept those hats in their boxes and that we buried those boxes deeply and forever. It was always up to them.

 # SEPARATION

THERE IS NO SECURITY ON
THIS EARTH; THERE IS ONLY
OPPORTUNITY.
—General Douglas MacArthur

As a new parent, I did not see
the relationship between summer camp for the first time and
college campus for the first time. But as the years stretched on,
my children taught me that these two unique environments are
indeed related. One of them, summer camp, taught my children
how to succeed in the other, the college campus, and how to
enjoy a productive educational experience.

When I left my firstborn seven-year-old son at a summer
camp for the first time, I struggled. As a young boy, he enjoyed
many weekend outings—with grandma and grandpa, cousins,
and friends. But camp was his first extended separation (three
weeks) from mom and dad. We prepared well ahead of time.
We shopped for the appropriate camp items and used the
official list as our guide. Twelve pair of socks. Check. Seven pair
of underwear. Check. Two pair of jeans. Check. Four T-shirts.
Check. One bathing suit. Check. Stationery and stamps. Check,
check.

The stationery and stamps were to be used by him but *really* were for me. Handwritten letters were the only means of communication I would have for the duration, and they were the only way for me to learn if he was having a good time. Was he making friends? Which of the many camp activities did he sign up for? Were the counselors nice? How was the food? I was eager to read his scribbled answers to these questions and more.

My husband and I emptied our permanent marking pens identifying our son's things—socks, shirts, shorts, hairbrush, toothbrush, and flashlight—as being solely his. (How he returned with a duffle bag filled with other people's clothing and paraphernalia still baffles me.) My husband packed his son's travel bag as no one else on Earth could have. One end became the toiletry section—shampoo, toothpaste, and soap. The opposite end housed the nighttime needs—pajamas, sweat shirt, and jacket. The middle top was dedicated to daytime clothing—shorts, T-shirts, and socks. The middle bottom accommodated the towels, books, and items of great significance—like stationery, stamps, and pens.

We packed the car, drove two and a half hours, arrived at the camp, and entered my son's assigned bunkhouse. My husband's task was to empty the orderly duffle bag he had just finished packing and reorganize the contents in their new but temporary location, a beat-up cubby that sat next to my son's bed. Choosing the bed was critical—to me. Close to the counselors, but not too close. Bottom bunk, not top bunk (in case he rolled over in his sleep and fell out of bed). Near a window, but not right under a window. My son looked totally disinterested as I focused my energy on the proper bed assignment. He was too busy sizing up the other nine boys who would be his "pack" members over the next three weeks.

The bed was made (by throwing a sleeping bag and pillow onto a naked mattress), the towels were hung over the front of the cubby, the clothes and other belongings were organized in and around his space. There was nothing else for my husband

and me to do. That meant—oh, no—we had to say goodbye. Instead we decided to delay. We desperately sought out other tasks. "Let's help this other family organize their stuff. Let's introduce ourselves and our son to the other camper families." We postponed our exit as long as we could. But finally, the counselors kicked us out. This was the moment. The separation was inevitable. The time had come. I tried to hide the tears welling up in my eyes, but I don't think I was very successful. I lingered as I watched my son sitting on the edge of his bed. He looked alone. He looked small. He looked vulnerable. He looked ready. He looked brave. No tears in his eyes. I turned my back and left.

I left because I knew that camp was going to be a learning and maturing experience for him. I left because I knew he was in a safe and enriching environment. My husband and I first met at the college division of this camp, so I felt certain my son was in a good place. We knew he was going to be surrounded by hugs and laughter. We knew he was going to participate in the arts, outdoor activities, and meaningful conversations late into the night. We knew how loving his counselors were going to be. He was going to bond with a group of peers who shared the experience with him. He was going to learn to depend on counselors and himself—instead of his parents. He was going to learn to work things out on his own—without mom and dad rushing to the rescue. In short, he was going to prepare himself for the inevitable separation that was going to take place when he turned 18.

My husband and I returned home, prepared to face *our* learning and maturing experience, three weeks without our sweet seven-year-old son. We missed his presence, and we eagerly waited for a letter. After all, we had mailed our first letters to him before we even delivered him to camp.

Well, we waited. And we waited. And we waited. What did the time lag mean? Is he alive? Is he well? The camp would have notified us if anything was wrong. Week 1 passed. No camp mail. Week 2 passed. Again, no camp mail. I stoically reminded myself that this was my son's summer, not mine. Be patient, I told myself, and think this through. The lack of correspondence only means that he is having too much fun to write. In the middle of Week 3, when we were preparing to pick him up, it happened. An envelope arrived with "Mom and Dad" roughly scrawled on the front. I ran into the house and ripped the letter open. I saw two hurried sentences scribbled on a crumpled piece of paper: "Having a great time and making lots of friends. Got to go."

I sighed with relief. Those two sentences told me everything I needed to know. He was making friends. He was happy. He was busy—too busy to take the time to correspond with his family back home. He was bonding. He was playing. He was learning. *And he was successfully preparing to leave us one day.*

When we picked him up at the end of the session, he barely had time to say hello. After all, his counselor wanted a hug. And, camp style, it couldn't be just any old hug. My son had to run to the top of a hill, roll down to the bottom, and then jump into his counselor's waiting arms. My son made friends to keep in contact with, and a best friend who was part of our lives for many years to come. He did it—the camp experience—and he did it successfully. He was beaming with delight at his achievements. He had accomplished so much and learned so much—about himself. Yes, people liked him—counselors and campers alike. Yes, he liked so many different types of people in return. Yes, he was able to bond deeply with others over a three-week period of time. Yes, he was able to risk (sneaking out of the bunk at night to raid the kitchen) and survive. Yes, he was capable of making it on his own—without depending on Mom and Dad. Yes, he learned exciting things about art, dance, nature, culture, history, and tradition. And yes, he wanted to go back and do it again, year after year after year, as did all of my children.

Never again did I say goodbye to my summer campers with tears in my eyes. I knew that while they were away, they would enjoy many significant personal triumphs. These achievements were critical to building the confident, courageous, and prepared 18-year-olds who so easily and eagerly separated from their home environment to start college adventures. I learned to let go, to realize that each of my children had lessons to learn independent of what I had to teach them. My love for them inspired me to loosen my hold so that they could eventually learn to fly from the nest.

When my children were college freshmen, they witnessed separation anxiety in others. Some gave in to it and decided to remain home. Others left home for an out-of-town school but didn't last a full quarter. Still others let themselves and their parents down by choosing not to pursue a goal they were once passionate about.

Many of the college freshmen my kids encountered were experiencing freedom for the first time. They frequented the party scenes loaded with alcohol, drugs, or whatever else allowed them to express that they could make their own decisions now. Others advertised individuality and rebelliousness with attitudes they never would have expressed at home. Some called their parents daily because they had trouble detaching and needed to touch base on a regular basis. And on and on and on.

In contrast, my children *eagerly* took on the challenges of their freshman year. They delighted in choosing their courses and planning their lives, and they stayed to make the best of it. They disdained the party scene. I could hear it in their voices when they described what was going on in the streets at night. They demonstrated no rebellious signs because they had already discovered who they were, summer after summer, in a safe camp setting (and at home, as well). They didn't call home every day—nor did I call them. When they left for college, I merely said, "Call me whenever. Don't worry about it." Basically, that meant, "Go ahead and handle your life. Overcome your challenges. Learn to figure things out on your own. But I'm still here if you need me."

The ability my children developed to steer their course didn't mean that my husband and I were absent during times of need. Cars break down and checks are written. Relationships break up, and sympathetic ears are sought. Life directions are considered, and opinions are solicited. But the daily struggles of making it on their own were conquered by my children. Normally, they handled things first and called me later.

The calls I received from my college-age children were almost always about sharing exciting events in their lives. This one got a 95 percent on his final. This one wrote a paper that the professor read in class. This one involved herself in a club or activity. This one "met someone." This one stood up for this, that, or the other thing.

The ease with which my children assimilated into their college lifestyles was remarkable to me. The three weeks they spent at summer camp had been constructive. Separation from Mom and Dad at an appropriate time and age into a loving environment helped our children gain confidence, independence, and maturity. Camp helped my children make hard-knock decisions and develop pride in their ultimate survival. Separation led to victory in my children's lives. It left them with a sense of comfort and satisfaction in knowing they could make it on their own.

I advise parents to get out their permanent marking pens. Start IDing those socks. Send your children on their summer camp way. Temporarily loosen your grip. Know that your children are in a safe environment. Let them benefit from the lessons new role models have to teach them. Let them develop their social skills as they move quickly from knowing no one else to bonding closely to almost everyone else. Let them be introduced to new skills and new schedules. But don't mope around the house waiting for a letter to arrive. Your child may be too engaged and too proud of his newfound independence to realize you, his parents, are struggling with separation anxiety.

SEX AND DRUGS

IN THE ART OF LOVE IT
IS MORE IMPORTANT TO
KNOW WHEN THAN HOW.

When I was a young mom, I often reflected on child-rearing issues that might come up in the years ahead. When I thought about the topics of sex and drugs, I usually imagined teenage angst, experimentation, and rebellion. Sex and drugs were big topics for me, as they are for most parents because they extended beyond the realm of family values. They have the potential to affect children's health and safety as well. Just thinking about what I could be in for gave *me* angst. Would my children make wise decisions, even if Mom and Dad were not there to monitor them? One thing I knew for sure was this: These subjects were not going to come up for the first time when my children were hormonally crazed adolescents who were sneaking around or screaming "Why not?" and "Everybody else is doing it."

Not long ago, I heard a mother talking on the radio. She was asking for advice regarding her recently traumatized nine-year-old daughter. Her daughter's innocence had been carefully guarded by her parents throughout her childhood, and the girl knew absolutely nothing about sex: what it is, what it's for, and within what context it should be expressed. As often happens when children play with other children, the subject of sex came up, and the girl was exposed by a playmate to a raw picture of a live sex act. The result was a shaken-up nine-year-old girl who ran home to her mother in complete shock.

That public radio conversation brought back memories. I smiled as I recalled the day I came home from elementary school and asked my mother the definition of a graphic sex term I had heard. She didn't miss a beat. She continued working in the kitchen. She gave me an accepting smile. She responded with a simple and honest answer that was appropriate for my age. She waited to see if I had any other questions, which I did not. Then she watched me make an about-face to run outside and play. I was not there to see her reaction after I left. So I don't know if she slumped in a chair heaving a sigh, broke out in a cold sweat, or burst out laughing. But from my vantage point at the time, she was as cool as the cucumber she was slicing. And I am so grateful for that. I experienced no trauma and no devastation. We didn't have to hold a family conference or meet with a psychologist. I just filed away her answer in my elementary-school brain and went outside to play.

I understand a parent's desire to protect the innocence of their children. But I didn't want my kids to be protected from sex in a way that taught them to fear sexual contact in a morally safe environment. Nor did I want them to abuse sexual contact without restraint. I chose to introduce the subject slowly, over time, so that questions could be asked and answered and appropriate choices could be made—each in their own time. I planned my strategy so that the kids could benefit from as much information, and suffer as little trauma as possible.

My children learned about sex and drugs at a very early age. Their education started when they were probably two or three years old and continued for years—until they ran out of questions and they were on their own. There was never a big sex talk, just a series of lessons here and lessons there. And it all started with a book—a children's book called *Where Did I Come From?* by Peter Mayle. The subtitle was "The facts of life without any nonsense and with illustrations." No nonsense—just my style. With illustrations—just their style.

The book was placed on my children's bookshelf right between Dr. Seuss's *ABC* book and *The Little Engine that Could*. It was nothing unusual, nothing out of the ordinary. It was just another book that the kids could pull off of their shelf and ask Mom or Dad to read to them at night. The book was charming and adorably illustrated. It was honest and age appropriate. It talked about how "little people are made by bigger people," not by storks and not by fairies. It discussed the differences between male and female bodies, "romantic" sperm, tickling sensations, and how one egg develops from a speck to a baby in nine months.

The kids listened calmly and attentively as I read this book the exact same way I read any other book. Why were they so accepting? Because the subject was presented very naturally, and it spoke to them at their age level. There was no embarrassment. They did not hesitate to ask questions, and I did not hesitate to answer them—simply and briefly. If the first short answer did the trick, we moved on to another page or another topic. If they were ready for a more complex answer, they asked the next question and received the next response. I never volunteered more than their childhood brains could handle at any particular moment.

I did not teach the subject of sex education to all three of my kids in a group setting. The reason? They were each in a different stage of readiness. This book was read to one child at a time—privately. I did not want a three-year-old learning about sex at a ten-year-old level. Nor did I want sex to be the topic of conversation at the family dinner table. Sex was private and personal, and that is how we discussed it. Openly, fluently, comfortably—but privately.

Teaching sex education to my children at a young age

benefited them in many ways. First and foremost, I was able to introduce an "Aharoni family code" of morals and ethics. I could slip in lessons on commitment, self-discipline, respect for others, marriage, and loyalty. I could influence my children never to take advantage of another human being in order to get something they wanted, and I could impact their future decision making by discussing the beauty of physicality in a relationship that is long term and monogamous.

Conversely, I could open up the Pandora's box of possible complications that can result from sexual contact, whether that be monogamous and long-term or uncommitted and superficial: unwanted pregnancies; sexually transmitted diseases (STDs); and feelings of being left, ignored, hurt, or used. All of these things were open season during our bedtime readings and conversations. I admitted when pressed that it is possible for a teenager to engage in sex and suffer none of these problems, but I emphasized that both physical and emotional complications were much more likely with sexual activity than without.

My goal was a simple one: to get my children through high school and to the age of legal maturity (18) without engaging in sex or indulging in drugs. Why 18? One, my legal responsibility to my children ended at 18. As legal adults, any mistakes my children made would be their responsibility to solve or suffer. Two, the law in my state backed me up. Statutory rape laws address children under the age of 18. And three, I thought that most children under the age of 18 did not have the maturity or life experience to make the wisest choices. I hoped that by the time my kids were 18, out of the house, and on their own, I would have been able to help them absorb enough information and behavioral guidelines to support them in making their own sensible decisions—for a lifetime.

The subject of drugs was addressed the same way as the topic of sex. Though I did not have a cute little book to refer to, the topic was raised at a very young age. Questions were asked. Answers were given. Rules of behavior were discussed. Complications were dealt with.

It was not enough for me to say that drugs are bad. Children want to know in respect to what. So my husband and I discussed our goals for our children. We wanted them to be healthy, safe, independent, and productive. Examples were introduced of people who had contributed to society in a healthy, positive way and others who had wasted time in chemical self-absorption. Lessons were taught about the benefits of tackling challenges head on with a clear mind and the disadvantages of escaping and hiding from reality. Conversations were held about promoting personal safety versus driving while impaired (along with other safety issues). Discussions were introduced about respecting your health and honoring your body versus smoke and pills and emergency rooms. And instruction was given about the freedom that is enjoyed when one follows the law versus the constricting consequences that are suffered after one breaks the law.

Unlike the topic of sex, drugs were discussed around the dinner table and in a group setting. With all three children present, we were able to get some vital and healthy conversations flowing. We talked, for example, about the importance of children filling their needs—health and safety needs, social needs, physical needs, and psychological needs—within the family's guidelines and society's laws. We further spoke about how filling these needs through clubs, social activities, athletics, creative pursuits, and release (or control) of emotions was healthier than gravitating to a drug-induced solution, loneliness, or feeling misunderstood.

And so it went in the Aharoni home. Books were read. Questions were asked. Answers were given. Discussions were held. No preaching. No threatening. Just an easy stream of information with an added dose of our particular moral convictions.

As far as I know, we have had no pregnancies, no STDs, and no drug abuse. None of my children ever intentionally used or mistreated another human being. They never coerced someone into doing something they didn't want to do for a few moments of physical pleasure, and they never gave in in order to fit in.

None of this would have worked if my children didn't respect my husband and me. Our children worked hard to make their mom and dad pleased with their lifestyles, their efforts, and their choices. Nothing seemed to be as important to them as having their parents feel pride and admiration in their behavior. Their dignity, honor, and self-respect were predicated on this.

So success with sex education and drug education turned out to be about a few specific things: our parent-child relationship, an information flow, openness to questions, and a code of conduct. Because we started early, we had just enough time to complete the process by the time the kids turned 18.

My mother paved the way for me with regard to sex and drug education. And for a while she was there to contribute to her grandchildren's education as well. One of my fondest memories is of the day my mother's newest grandchild, who was about two at the time, begged her to read him a book. Hand in hand, they approached the bookshelf. Together they lowered themselves onto the floor. "This one," he said. He pulled out the book with the caricature of the naked little baby on the front cover. "Fine," she responded. The next time I saw them, he was cuddled in her lap on a lounge chair in our backyard. They were reading the sex book and having a wonderful time. When they were done, he ran off to play, and she reentered the house laughing. "I did not expect that," she said.

I doubt my mother remembered my question of so long ago. But history was repeating itself in a very loving and relaxed way. I appreciated her openness and honesty to me so many years ago. And because of her reactions to my questions, I was able to be open and honest with my children as well.

The topics of sex and drugs do not have to be traumatic, and they do not have to be huge. I started when my kids were young, and I kept it age appropriate. I was patient. I let things progress at their own speed. My husband and I sprinkled in our values. My kids were on their way.

By the time sex and drugs were novel and exciting topics to

schoolyard friends, they were old-hat topics for my children. My kids already had the knowledge my husband and I had given them, and they already absorbed the values we had instilled. The process had been painless and fluid. Our 18-year plan contributed so much to the wise decisions my children have made throughout their lifetimes.

SLEEP

THE HARDEST THING IN
THE WORLD TO RAISE IS A
CHILD—ESPECIALLY IN THE
MORNING.

Certain scientific theories say that
the human need for sleep is even greater than the human need
for food. In other words, if your impoverished and fatigued
body were presented with a choice of food or sleep, sleep would
be the better choice. The renewal of your body through sleep
would clear your mind and restore your physical self, which, in
turn, would improve your chances of finding or earning food.
A new parent who gets a few solid hours of uninterrupted
sleep can be more patient, understanding, and perceptive than
one who is sleep deprived. Realizing this, my husband and I
thought long and hard about sleep and how we could use it to
be the best parents we were capable of being—all day, every
day.

After my babies were born, I was empathetic with the school
of thought that said newborns cannot be spoiled, only loved.
And I appreciated that exploding into the world the way babies
do is exhausting and traumatic and that infants need touch and

comfort and cuddling to feel secure. And I valued the fact that there is no heaven on earth like the warmth of an infant's body stretched across your torso, limp with slumber, sucking in tiny breaths of air. But I also recognized that these little angels were capable of engaging in long-term, tiring, and wakeful struggles with their sleep-deprived parents.

When I looked into my first-born's bassinet through sleep-encrusted eyes, I realized that I did not want parent-child struggles to continue later on with a teenager who was bigger than I, quicker than I, and stronger than I. I knew that I needed to establish myself as an authority figure when my children were young—very young. Their respect for me would diminish the domestic tumult of teenage testing. I was certain there were many challenges ahead. But the sleep test was the one that I had to deal with first. I had to lay down some ground rules to ensure that each family member got some regular, replenishing sleep.

Babies cry. Sometimes they cry for a legitimate reason. But other times they cry because they have learned that this small effort on their part can bring them immediate results—the presence of Mom or Dad. Immediate gratification is good—in the baby's mind. But not for the mom or dad who is stumbling out of bed, bleary eyed, worn out, and sleep deprived—again. "If I could just get four hours of uninterrupted rest . . . ."

For several weeks after my babies were born (maybe four to eight weeks depending on the size, strength, and health of the newborn), I was at the mercy of my children. I sacrificed myself completely for their needs. I gave them time to acclimate to the home environment, to become accustomed to the family voices and the household routine. As this practice proceeded, I reflected on what I wanted from my children in the future. I wanted them to be emotionally and physically healthy *and* independent. In other words, I wanted my children to come to me for help when they legitimately needed it—*after* they had tried to solve their problems on their own.

So when I felt my baby had reached a level at which he should have been able to sleep soundly for three to four hours on four-plus ounces of milk, I began to suspect the genuineness of his hourly "hunger" cry. I drew a soft line in the sand. Would I instantly and helplessly surrender to my baby's demanding cry, or could he move a bit closer to my objective, which was having *all* family members get some uninterrupted sleep? Does he really need to eat every hour all night long, or is he merely availing himself of a human pacifier?

About the time my baby's stomach was large enough to hold four-plus ounces of milk was about the time I felt it should get empty enough to take four-plus ounces of milk—not one ounce here (followed by snoring) and one ounce there (followed by more snoring). I preferred not to continuously "top him off" because that routine was playing havoc with *my* healing process, *my* ability to parent, and *my* relationship with my husband.

Daytime was easy. When my infant cried, I distracted him with music, dancing, reading (yes, I read to my newborns), and playing (me playing, him tolerating being played with). I put him in my Snuggly (close-to-the-chest baby carrier) and got projects done. If he started crying in his bed after a feeding, I let him hear my voice and sense my proximity. I then took a minute or two to finish whatever I was doing before approaching him. My focus was to attend to him, but not to trip over my feet rushing to him. We were both going to have to be patient when it came to filling needs.

The nights definitely needed a plan. The first step of the night plan was confirming that the baby was not crying for a legitimate reason like hunger, pain (from the diaper pins of those days), a dirty diaper, or fear (of a loud sound or an unfamiliar light). Once that was determined, my strategy progressed in minutes. If the baby fussed in the middle of the night, I stayed in bed. Sometimes a fuss was just a fuss—not a prelude to an outburst. If the fuss developed into an all-out wail, on Day 1 of the plan, I let him cry for one minute before I picked him up. On Day 2, I let him cry for two minutes. On Day 3, I let him cry for three minutes. And so on. Before I ever came near approaching 10 minutes, I had reached my goal. My four- to eight-week old infant was enjoying a four-hour stretch of sleep. My baby was learning that I would always be there to comfort him, but not exclusively on his terms.

The next step was scheduling. I discovered that six hours of sleep was what I needed to function properly as a parent during the day and what my husband needed to perform properly at work. In order to accomplish this lofty goal, I went to sleep very early. By 8 P.M. I was in bed and snoozing. My husband fed our babies one bottle a day, so he took the feeding that usually occurred around 10 P.M. This one bottle enabled us to accomplish all of our sleep goals. I was able to enjoy six hours of uninterrupted sleep between 8 P.M. and 2 A.M., which was about the time the baby woke up for a feeding. My husband enjoyed a rejuvenating sleep between 10 P.M. and 6 A.M., which was the time he woke up for work. And the baby was able to enjoy some invigorating rest and some bonding with parents who were ready, willing, and able to relate to him.

When my kids were one to two months old, I encouraged them to sleep a little longer by adding a little rice cereal to Dad's 10 P.M. bottle (Grandma's advice). Like magic, that little extra bulk helped the baby sleep longer. (Please talk to your pediatricians before even thinking about trying this out. We put this into practice a long time ago when the rules were very different than they are today.) By six weeks old or so, the babies were sleeping a good six hours. I was sleeping, and my husband was sleeping. By three months old, the babies were out for the night. At that point, the children were moved out of our bedroom and into their own space (so my husband and I could feel like a couple again). Intercom systems were set in place, and the nights were peaceful and healing—for all of us. We no longer suffered the hazy, crazy, frazzled, hassled days and nights we heard other new parents had experienced for a year or longer.

The "three-months-and-you're-out-of-our-bedroom" rule brings me to a topic I alluded to earlier—the marriage relationship. I have often said to young parents that *the best thing you can do for your children is have a happy marriage*. I wanted desperately to spare my kids the childhood pain of parental separation and divorce. I was not willing to let this new member of the family push our marital bond into a dark and receding place. It was important to me to take my bedroom and my loving relationship back—and also to enjoy an evening out once in a while on a twilight date. It was vital (for the baby) that my husband and I reconnect as partners, lovers, and friends. It was critical that I continue to take care of my husband and he continue to take care of me so we both could continue to take care of the kids. For example, if we were in the car on a short trip, I normally sat in the front seat by my husband. I was confident my children would survive the trip locked in the safety of their backseat car seats. But how long would my marriage have survived if my husband and I grew to ignore our honored positions in each other's lives?

After our children were born, my husband went through disruptions and emotional ordeals, just like I did. And even though he was a man who expressed himself differently from his female counterpart, he had feelings and needs too. As a wife, I showed appreciation to my husband for all the ways he was supporting and protecting me and his family. I told him and showed him often (as he did to me). I never felt that this newborn experience was about any one member of the family. I felt it was about *every* member of the family. It was a time for us to work together, to value each other, to negotiate, and to make concessions—in order to get everyone's needs met. All this was done with one goal in mind—a family unit that would move forward with love, respect, generosity, and commitment.

Lessons can be learned in a variety of settings—even on an airport runway. Flight attendants regularly tell us, "If the oxygen masks release from the ceiling, place a mask on your face before you place a mask on the child seated next to you." The message here is that adults need to take care of themselves before they can efficiently and effectively take care of those who are completely dependent upon them. I encourage new parents not to ignore their own needs as they throw themselves into the all-consuming task of infant care and not to ignore their spouses. Yes, a dependent baby's legitimate needs come first, but you will be much more able to satisfy those needs in a warm and patient manner if you have had a little sleep and if your partner feels loved and welcomed into your growing family circle.

START YOUNG

BABIES ARE SUCH A NICE
WAY TO START PEOPLE.
–DON HEROLD

Do you want to discipline a strong-willed, stubborn, independent teenager who thinks he is always right? One who is constantly exasperated because no one understands his need to assert himself? Or would you rather discipline a strong-willed, stubborn, independent toddler who thinks she is always right? One who also is constantly exasperated because no one understands her need to assert herself? Huhm! I choose the toddler—hands down.

My choice to discipline my toddlers was actually a choice *not* to discipline my teenagers. With toddlers, I had a physical advantage: height, weight, and strength. In addition, they still viewed me as a protector, a support, and an ally. If a toddler didn't want to get with the discipline program, I could pick him up and place him in his room. If a teenager didn't want to get with the program, I had to depend on the credibility I had built as a parent up to that point and hope that my past behavior could influence his future conduct.

Toddlers and teenagers have a lot in common. Both groups are moving from one stage of life to another. Toddlers are moving from babyhood to childhood, and teenagers are moving from childhood to young adulthood. Advancing from one phase to another requires courage, confidence, and commitment. But it also involves fear, insecurity, and anxiety. When you throw all of these ingredients into the child-rearing pot, parents have a major challenge on their hands during these critical phases of growth and development.

When my kids were small, this was my attitude: If I take care of my parental business while my children are young, I won't have to battle with them during their angst-filled, hormone-driven teenage years, when the consequences will be more serious and the threat to their health and well-being will be higher. After all, it is easier to deal with a tantrum in the middle of Macy's toy department than it is to deal with a teenager who stays out all night doing who-knows-what with a group of high school buddies. Most teenagers will test their boundaries, no matter what home environment they grow up in. My hope was that if I played my cards right, my children's tests would be manageable for them, for me, and for the entire family. All of us could have happily survived a new and offbeat haircut, outfit, or friend. But illegal, violent, or underage behavior would have opened up an entirely different and all-consuming can of worms.

Once I decided to start disciplining my children when they were young, I debated with myself about the benefits of being the nice guy versus the strict disciplinarian. I decided on the following approach: to build my credibility with my children (so that I could draw on it in the future) and to balance being tough and consistent (when appropriate) with being understanding and loving (when appropriate). Building credibility meant building respect, and I felt my children could learn to respect me if I represented the law of the household *fairly, powerfully, and consistently.* Here are some of the ideas and practices I utilized:

Justice: "But that's not fair" are words children learn to use early and frequently. And they are words I felt I needed to consider. Justice was important in our household, and that meant everyone had a right to be heard. Yes, I was the acting judge and jury, and I was the one who announced the verdict. But I always encouraged my children to represent themselves in my courtroom. After all, I probably would not have been able to gather all of the evidence on my own—without their input.

For example, let's say one of my children decided to create a colorful crayon collage *on the living room wall*—a fact. My first reaction could have been to teach her how to wipe the slate clean with some good old fashioned elbow grease. Afterward, I may have decided to take away the crayons for the rest of the day. As I stood with my hands on my hips viewing Exhibit A, that response may have seemed fair. But what if I asked my child why she decided to decorate the walls? And what if her response was that she wanted to make something pretty for me? The elaborate wall design was a gift of love—a present for me.

At that point I would have had to consider if I wanted my sentence to reflect retribution (punishment) or rehabilitation (helping her choose not to engage in the same behavior in the future). Since I felt it was fair to reserve punishment for intentional misdeeds or character issues, and to soften my stance when aiming for behavioral changes, a solution to the crayon dilemma might have looked something like this: an expression of gratitude for the loving thoughts, an explanation of why we don't write on walls, a suggestion of an alternative way to deliver the message, and an agreement that she is welcome to draw, but only on paper. There might have been a brief warning that if the paper rule was breached, a consequence would follow. With this approach, I could acknowledge her motivation for the act, offer an alternative solution, allow her to feel the pinch of her decorating deed, and teach her a lesson about respecting the family walls. Sounds fair to me.

Power: If I didn't deliver my discipline messages powerfully and confidently to my children, I would have set myself up to be mowed down by little people who had no qualms about asserting *their* power in commanding ways. Actually, asserting themselves was a skill I wanted my children to learn, but with self-controlled confidence and certainty, not with self-indulgent declarations and demands. After all, assertiveness demonstrates spirit—a crucial component to future success. My children knew that asserting themselves did not mean getting their way. As a parent, I celebrated their bold attempts to influence me, but I also maintained my standards authoritatively and unwaveringly.

Let's take a past trip to Grandma's house as an example. Grandma and Grandpa were waiting for us to arrive. Grandma was busy cooking favorite dishes and filling her candy jar. Grandpa was busy running the vacuum and cleaning the yard. On my end, everyone was dressed, hair was combed, and hands were clean. I announced, "It's time to get in the car." But my toddler had another idea: "No! I don't want to." At this point I had a couple of options, I could have begged, pleaded, and bribed. But if I did, what would my child have learned? 1) that he could reduce me to a heap of beseeching flesh, 2) that King-Little-One had complete control, and 3) that I was at *his* mercy.

Instead, I decided to teach him that the Queen ruled this castle. I slowly and deliberately approached him, determined to instill the fear of Mom in him. I bent down to his level, looked straight into his eyes, used my voice at a controlled decibel level, placed my finger on his cheek, and demanded what I demanded—that he get in the car. At this point he knew I meant business, and he could either do what I had asked or make another mutinous attempt. If he tried it again (as he did in this case), I picked him up, put him in his room, and let him know that if he didn't cooperate within three minutes, I was going to call a babysitter, and we were going to leave without him. Three minutes later, if he insisted on sticking to his guns (which he didn't), the babysitter would have been called, and *we would have, in fact, left without him.*

I only had to use this technique (leaving a child behind) at its maximum level once for each of my kids. And that one time was when they were young, probably between the ages of four and six. As soon as they got the message that I meant what I said, they chose from then on to surrender at Level 1.

Consistency: If I had asserted my position on Monday, but decided on Tuesday that I was too tired and time challenged to follow through with steadfastness and force, I would have abdicated my position. Consistency was the mortar that held our structure together. My duty was to raise children who could make decisions that benefited themselves, their families, and their society. If they were led to believe that they could get whatever they wanted just because they wanted it, the family walls could easily have started to crack and fall.

For example, if one day I insisted that my child take a bath—against his wishes—but then I gave in the next day and let the bath slide, I would have opened the door to a political takeover. My toddler kids, like most toddler kids, were smart and tenacious. They perceived moods and detected weaknesses. No matter how I felt on the second day, I had to force myself from the comfort of my couch and gather my strength for the bubble bath battle ahead. I had to be fair. I had to be powerful. And I had to insist—every single time.

As these many small clashes were occurring, they may not have seemed worth the energy I was expending. But expend it I did—early and often. The benefit was that as my children grew older, I was exerting less and less effort. Soon I began to enjoy my kids with an ease that I had only dreamed of in the past.

I always tell people who ask me about discipline that I did all of my disciplining when my children were young, starting at toddlerhood and continuing through preschool and early elementary school. I was fair. I was powerful. And I was consistent. When we were in the middle of an episode, I didn't care if my children responded to my requests out of fear, respect, or a combination of the two. But I learned over time that my children, indeed, did grow to respect me. And the choices they made as young adults ensured that I continued to respect them.

We suffered very few cracks in our family walls as my children proceeded through grammar school, junior high, high school, and college. Our structure was built out of bricks—not sticks. I nurtured our home from the ground up. The process was not effortless. It took the creativity and wisdom of a good architect (to design the plans). And it took the strength and perseverance of a good carpenter (to implement the plans). But the end result was one we could all live with and enjoy—brick by brick and room by room.

TEACH THEM TO ARGUE

THERE IS NOTHING SO
EXASPERATING AS
ARGUING WITH SOMEONE
WHO KNOWS WHAT HE'S
TALKING ABOUT.

Because I was an uncertain and introverted child, I wanted to teach my children to *confidently* reason through issues, acquire a point of view, and stand up for themselves. Knowing how to successfully argue your case is important—at home, at school, at work, and with peers. By "successfully," I do *not* mean victoriously. I mean the ability to artfully use skills that have been developed and polished over time. Yes, I wanted my children to do what I asked them to do, but I never required them to be automatons. I wanted them to express their opinions, ideas, and feelings—and to feel safe doing so. Even though I was a monarchal ruler, my decisions were made after receiving input from all interested parties.

My children were welcomed and encouraged to dispute stands I took, to make counterclaims, and to present opposing points of view. But just as every courtroom adheres to certain rules, we abided by a set of laws in our "courthouse." Presentations were to be based on reason, not pure emotion.

Presenters were to show respect to all other parties at all times. And the "judge's" final decision was just that—final. Appeals were not accepted.

The courthouse process started when the children were young, bouncy, and full of energy. Here is an example of what might have transpired: *I* wanted my kids to stay indoors until 10 A.M. on the weekends so as not to disturb our sleeping neighbors. The *kids* wanted to go outside and test the limits of their new roller skates or practice a new skateboard trick. I made my opening statement: "You will play indoors until 10 A.M." They countered with this: "You are always telling us that we need sunshine and exercise. We won't be able to play outside later because we are going to visit aunts, uncles, and cousins. It's boring in the house. We'll be quiet outside." Et cetera.

The ball was now in my court: "There is plenty of sunshine and exercise at your aunt and uncle's house. Your cousins will be there to help you move and soak up the rays. If you think about it for a few minutes, you will probably discover that there is plenty to do in this house until 10 o'clock. It's impossible to be quiet outside with skates and skateboards."

They made another stab at it. I deflected the challenge. And the process continued until both sides were ready to mediate a solution.

At that point in the arbitration, it was important for me to keep an open mind and to proceed in the spirit of cooperation. What good was developing their reasoning skills if I didn't give them some type of reward at the end of the process? They needed to feel that their presentation made some measure of impact on me, because that impact was going to build their confidence and encourage them to expand their skills in the future.

I offered a potential solution to our standoff. They did the same. One option was to allow them to play outside with limits: in our yard only and without skates or skateboards. Play had to be limited to something quiet, like painting or Legos. The other option was to stay indoors but be able to do something active and loud, like holding a wrestling match.

I wanted the neighbors to get some weekend rest. The *kids* wanted to blow off some early-morning steam. They conferred. We discussed it and agreed. A wrestling match it was. We moved some furniture to create a "ring." We added a bell and a timer. Voila! We had a wresting match—and a solution.

The kids didn't get the sunshine, skates, or skateboard that they wanted. I didn't get the quiet that I preferred. But the neighborhood outside of our four walls was peaceful—my bottom line. The process was a rewarding one, and everyone was happy in the end. Especially me. I got to be the referee.

The skills my children developed through this "courthouse" process have served them well. For one, they have learned how to think. They were forced to use logic when they were young, and they have now become adept at applying it. "Because I want it" was never an acceptable argument in our household. Nor was "Because I said so" on my part (except in matters of health and safety).

My grown children have called on their reasoning abilities to choose schools and select careers. They have utilized their good-sense skills to select friends and build relationships. They have learned to think through issues and to develop counter arguments in all areas of their lives.

But none of that would have happened if my children had not learned to listen. At the same time I was bargaining with my kids, I was listening to them. And at the same time they were bargaining with me, they were listening to me. Serious thinking requires serious listening—being exposed to other points of view. By encouraging my children to think, I influenced them to listen. After all, the other party might have had a valid case to present. If that case was strong enough, it might have been worthy of acceptance or compromise. But if it was weak, it was open to penetration by another family member's logic and reason.

After the children listened attentively to my side of a story, it was their turn to fashion a response. This required quick thinking on their part. They had to understand the entirety of my case and discover its weaknesses. They had to break my argument into its component parts. This process proved to be great training for future educational achievements, social exchanges, and job advancement.

Boldness and tenacity were crucial when the children were articulating responses. If the kids were too frightened or meek to present their argument, they didn't have a chance to win a case or improve their standing through negotiation. Respect on both sides encouraged fortitude. Neither my husband nor I ever laughed at, made fun of, or humiliated a child who presented an argument or point of view (and vice versa). To do so would have discouraged them from future attempts.

My kids were sentient, responsive human beings with lots of spirit. To succeed in life, they needed to develop the fortitude to oppose what they felt was wrong, to accept what they felt was right, and to negotiate when appropriate—without regard to who presented whatever argument. Whether an idea came from within or from without, they needed to recognize it, deliberate over it, and act on it. I wanted my children to become contributors, movers, and shakers. But I also wanted them to be respected and honored for their insight, self-discipline, and ability to adjust.

Today my children have a highly developed sense of fairness and justice. They know, through many years of practice, that a reasonable solution can almost always be found. Because of this insight, my children have never claimed victimhood. Life's challenges were not simply happening *to* them. Ideas were identified, considered, and acted upon. My children were always invited to search for and be part of a potential solution. They grew and matured as a result.

Accepting the judge's final decision teaches an important lesson to young minds: You can't have everything you want whenever you want it. You may be offered 80 percent of whatever it is you are after, but if you push your case to the limit with unbendable stubbornness, you may end up with nothing at all.

A teenager who argues that he stay out until midnight, when his parents insist he be home by 10 P.M., could end up spending the entire evening in his room if he responds disrespectfully and emotionally. But if he makes his case civilly about the importance of the school activity and the number of adult supervisors who will be present, if he names his cohorts and delivers phone numbers where he can be reached, he may actually make it to 11 P.M. Though 11 P.M. is not everything he wanted, his reasoned approach won him something. Feeling melancholy about the hour he lost is easily offset by the pride he feels in the hour he gained.

Teaching my children to argue their case sharpened their ability to negotiate their way through life using logic, reason, and compromise. They learned to express what was important to them in a respectful and thoughtful way. And they learned, through listening, what was important to others. After all of the information was in, they were able to make decisions about what was worth pursuing and what was not, what was worth pushing to the limit, and what could have rebounded negatively. They learned to be thorough. They developed the spirit of taking on challenges. They negotiated their way through the middle-ground maze. They developed confidence—not arrogance. And their self-assurance was based on something real, something earned, not on empty platitudes and meaningless self-esteem builders.

Being able to argue and negotiate is not about winning or losing. It is about gaining the skills needed to succeed at work, at home, and at play. No matter what the outcome, a child who delivers a solid case and is open to opposing viewpoints is a winner every time.

CONCLUSION

> THE HAND THAT ROCKS
> THE CRADLE RULES THE
> WORLD.
> —WILLIAM ROSS WALLACE

As I turn out the light that is dangling over the keyboard that defines my writing space, I feel confident that I am qualified to write this book—even though I am not a psychiatrist, a psychologist, or a therapist. Nor am I an expert who is educationally trained to answer child-rearing questions or give professional advice. As a parent, I have had my vulnerabilities. I have made mistakes, been stretched to my limit, and blown my top.

When I ask myself why I feel entitled to write this book about my experiences, my choices, and my development as a parent, my answer is this: Because I have raised three good kids. And I have the evidence to prove it—I gave my children a goodness test.

A few years ago, I heard Dennis Prager (radio talk show host, philosopher, and theologian) lecture on the importance of goodness. He discussed how society benefits when parents concentrate on raising *good* children, as opposed to smart, successful, happy, or wealthy kids (or fill in the adjective of your choice). He suggested that we each give our children (young and old) a test to determine what *they* think *our* parental focus was while raising them.

It sounded interesting to me. So I did it. I contacted my three children and administered the test. They were young adults at the time. I was curious what their answers would be. As a parent, I hoped my children would develop many qualities—happiness, success, intelligence, et cetera—but goodness was the most precious to me. I was eager to know if I had passed that message on to my children.

The initial responses I received from all three of my children were laughter, followed by, "That's easy, Mom."

At that point I felt a little nervous. Were they going to say "successful"? Did they think I was most impressed by a large paycheck and a three-piece suit? Were they going to say "smart"? Did they think I was most interested in their IQ scores or a membership in MENSA? No. Here is what they said:

"You wanted us to be good."

"You wanted us to be good."

"You wanted us to be good."

It was three for three. But even so, how did I know that they each practiced a similar brand of goodness and decency—the type I tried to instill in them over the years? Simple. By observing their behavior.

They all have grown into adults who fill out school and employment applications honestly, rather than cheat to ensure themselves a better spot in line. They all return the extra change the cashier has mistakenly given them. They pay for the piece of fruit they are eating as they walk down the aisles of the grocery store. They offer a leftover sandwich to the homeless person sitting on the sidewalk. They are kind to people who are working hard in a variety of service industries. They volunteer in the community and help family and friends. They understand that every person is important and that their actions affect others.

It looks as though my "goodness" message got through. Whew!

All parents seem to suffer some level of insecurity as they navigate the muddy waters of child rearing. It is common for parents to query other moms and dads when they are raising their children. "How did you handle this situation?" "How did you get through that stage?" "Maxwell doesn't want to eat his vegetables." "Allison always makes a scene in the grocery store." Some parents go directly to experts for help. Others go to the bookstore. Many depend on the advice of family and friends. Still others follow a propensity to do what their parents did or, conversely, to do the opposite. This book is my response to numerous queries from numerous parents: "You have such good kids. How did you handle such-and-such?"

I am not the only parent to raise good children. Many other parents have done it. I know because I have met the youngsters—my friends' children, my children's friends, my nieces, my nephews, and other contacts and acquaintances. My children's answers to the test question above were not exclusive to our family. Many parents are qualified, and perhaps morally obligated, to share their experiences with others as I have done here.

After dedicating many early mornings to my computer and my thoughts, the parental events I experienced and the lessons I learned are now an open book. And because we each have our own "book" of experiences and lessons, we can help teach each other. I have acquired insight from my children, but also from many other surprising places.

One tidbit I unexpectedly picked up was from a very wise cab driver my husband and I met during a visit to New Orleans. The cab driver who transported us was colorful, astute, and dedicated to his family. After he discussed in detail his favorite Cajun recipes, this is what he said: "The hand that rocks the cradle rules the world." (excerpted from a poem by William Ross Wallace, 1819-1881)

Those who "rock the cradle" should be on a mission to raise

children who are good, kind, and caring, but also brave, confident and self-sufficient—children who can think through issues and decide the proper course to take...children who have the spirit to take on leadership roles and/or influence others...children who can balance their lives and avoid fanatical obsessions...children who are respectful of other's points of view, even when they disagree...children who are independent, trustworthy, and honest.

Of course we want our children to be professionally successful, well liked, financially independent, and happy. But the *world* will benefit most from children who are raised primarily to be good. Good children grow into individuals who bring humanity and security to a fragile world.

Evil exists, and there are many ways to combat it. We can fight it, arrest it, "treat" it, and understand it. *Or* we can avoid some of it by giving our children tools and reasons for being good, for having integrity, and for demonstrating character.

You don't have to be wealthy or smart to raise good children. But you do have to be consistent and have the courage to act as an authority figure. I urge parents to consider the lessons they are teaching. As you "rock the cradle," you are impacting the safety and security of others. So take a moment to ask yourself this question: "Am I raising the bully, the bullied, or the protector of innocent victims?"

There are no guarantees when it comes to child rearing. There are many dedicated parents who are puzzled by a "bad seed." And there are many neglected children who are kind and loving. I am not here to answer the anomalies of child rearing. But I am here to say that we can give it a *good* shot.

In this book, I am answering a question I have often asked myself, the same question that other people have continually asked me: "How did you raise three good kids?" If anyone can learn anything from my experiences, then I have succeeded in this project. But we each have to chart our own course. It is my hope that, through this book, parents will consider my experiences, toss them around, and come up with their own unique methods of raising children who will one day laugh at them and say, "That's easy, Mom. You wanted us to be good."

☀ FAMILY FEEDBACK

Here is the view from the other side of these pages. Please join me in welcoming my family members: Eitan, Ilan, Eyal, and Galia. They have all read the manuscript and have contributed distinct opinions and reactions. The information I have shared with you in this book has been enriched by their encouraging responses.

HUSBAND

> *"Take care of the children, and society will take care of the rest."*

A long time ago, my wife and I were children. We grew up, married, and had our own kids. Then poof! They were out on their own. We wondered, as most parents do, if we had done a good job. Today, we frequently hear these types of comments: "You are so lucky. Your children are so good."

Most parents proclaim that they did the best they could when they were raising their children. But when we see the same parents raising several kids in the same environment, we can't help but notice sibling differences. The first child might be doing great; the second one might be doing okay but struggling a bit; and the third one might be dependent on illegal substances and have a criminal record. How can we explain these differences?

Are the results attributable to the amount of effort the parents put in? Or is it really the luck of the draw?

When I speak about my children to others, I find myself choosing my words carefully. My kids are remarkable, and I am careful not to boast about their character or their achievements. In my effort to be humble, I often respond, "Well, one works in a hospital, another is a researcher (and mountain unicyclist), and the other is into justice." What I refrain from saying is, "My children love to learn. One of them is a medical doctor with a GI specialty, the other is finishing up a doctorate in Evolutionary Psychology (and is considered one of the best mountain unicyclists in the country), and the third has a promising future in law and writing. They all have good characters. They are unassuming and generous. And I have not had a serious challenge with any of them—not ever!"

My wife's book is a personal guide for parents. It focuses on raising good children. While credentialed professionals have written many books on this subject, few have approached the subject from the common-sense angle of a layperson who actually has raised good kids. When we accept the notion that bad luck is keeping our children from being good people, we have lost the character battle forever.

My wife's book, *My Goodness: My Kids* is, in a way, a documentary of cause and effect. It implores readers to contemplate and recognize which human values are paramount for our children to possess when we send them out into the world. Most important, the book, and its many unconventional ways, points to the correlation of parenting efforts with day-to-day values.

My Goodness: My Kids is filled with examples of personal exchanges between parents and children. These conversations connect seemingly unimportant daily events with life changing, values-based results.

—Eitan Aharoni

FIRSTBORN

"Empathy is your pain in my heart."

When my mother asked me to contribute a few words to the Appendix of her book, of course I was honored to do so. However, it took me about six months longer than my siblings to submit my essay to her. Why? The answer is simple. It's because I have kids.

Taking care of the kids (changing diapers, making bottles, running baths, reading books…) became my constant immediate priority. Sitting down at the computer to write my thoughts on parenting became something I was going to get to "as soon as I finished with the kids." My oldest is two years old now, and I am finally learning that I am not going to be "finished" for another 16 years or so.

When I became a father for the first time, I soon realized that parenthood—which literally happens overnight—became my primary responsibility, and will remain so for the next eighteen years or so of my life. Previous simple pleasures—like going to a movie with my wife, watching the news, or reading a book in bed—are quickly set aside and replaced with the often overwhelming joy of watching my children grow and feeling like I am having a positive influence on their lives.

For me, the transition from becoming a young adult to becoming a parent was a time of deep reflection on my childhood and on the types of parenting skills I felt had the most profound effect on me. I thought about the techniques and philosophies that most contributed to the type of person I am today. I then transferred those musings onto my children and thought about how I might best raise them. Many of the ideas that surfaced you have read in the previous chapters. But for me, the one theme that was central to all others is what I like to call "acknowledging the other." By that, I mean how the actions of one person affect the other people in his or her surroundings. Examples of acknowledging the other are:

- How a toddler having a tantrum in an otherwise quiet restaurant affects other patrons who are trying to enjoy a pleasant meal.
- How a teenager who forgets to call when he or she is running late affects his or her parents' evening.
- How a bully's name calling affects other children's self-esteem.
- And how a simple smile, a kind compliment, or a pat on the back can so easily turn someone's day around.

My parents have instilled in me a sense of my actions—for good and for bad—and how they affect the people around me. This was a great gift, and I intend to pass it on to my children.

I have often heard people say, "I learned from my parents how I do not want to raise my children." Ironically, I heard this same sentiment from my own parents' mouths; however, I feel just the opposite. Granted, I was a pretty good kid, but I can't think of a single instance where I ever thought "That is one thing I am not going to do when I have children." On the contrary, I feel that my mother and father have succeeded tremendously as parents. I feel fortunate to have their experiences to look back on while I continue the challenging process of raising good children.

My two boys are very unique. They are individuals in their own right. When I study them deeply, I see some of myself in them. And when I contemplate my parenting ability, I see some of my parents in me. As I reflect on this big picture, I have a comforting sense that I am doing something right, and that my kids are going to be okay.

—ILAN AHARONI

MIDDLE CHILD

> *"Some of my best thinking has*
> *been done upside down."*
> —EYAL AHARONI

Looking back, how can we know if we turned out okay because of our parents or in spite of them? A thorough answer would require a very unethical experiment. So instead, I'll venture a humble guess.

Prior to reading this book, most of the values that I inherited from my parents were completely transparent to me. But one that always stuck out like a sore thumb was trustworthiness. Trustworthiness? But that's so cliché! Admittedly so, but I mean the term in a very specific way. My parents made their trust in me a valuable commodity. So when I did something to make them lose trust in me, that knowledge in itself was all that was needed to motivate me to correct my behavior.

For example, in 5th grade I literally stole a cookie from the teacher's cookie jar. Mom explained that I had effectively stolen someone else's property and, as a result, she couldn't fully trust me to be honest or to respect other people's belongings. Something registered. You might know this experience as guilt. But any guilt I might have felt for a particular bad behavior was not forced upon me in the form of a "guilt trip" delivered retroactively. My parents knew better than to do that. Instead, they had already shown me in advance that there are many irreplaceable benefits to reap by being a trustworthy person.

In this case, my mom explained that I could gradually earn her trust back (as well as my skateboard) by showing her evidence of good deeds. And as a young boy, I of course wanted all the benefits I could get. So I quickly learned to regulate my behavior in order to secure their trust.

As an adult, I no longer need to test my boundaries in order to learn how to behave. And I no longer need to "think before I act" because my prosocial behavior has become largely automatic, a machine that runs by itself. What a sensible idea!

But there are lots of sensible ideas. It would be misleading to give you the impression that a little bit of sensibility is all it takes to turn a naive little boy into a wise man. Roald Dahl captured one of my mother's favorite sentiments when he said that "a little nonsense now and then is relished by the wisest men." In "motherese," that means that in between all the lessons to be learned, a baby bubble-bath dance or an operatic toothbrushing song can go a long way in the formation of a happy, healthy, good human being.

Of course, there are lots of ways—sensible and nonsensical—to raise a child, and probably none of them will solve all the world's problems. But however it is that my parents raised me, I wouldn't have it any other way. And I believe this legacy will continue, not only through the generations of their children, but through all of those who come in contact with these fundamental life principles.

—EYAL AHARONI

THE BABY

> *"Freedom rings where opinions clash."*
> −ADLAI STEVENSON

I am sitting outside a coffee shop on a beautiful summer day. I am sipping tea in our impossibly perfect suburban beach town and thinking about my childhood. I've been granted the honor of writing a chapter in my mother's book—a feat of hers that fills me with so much pride at the thought of her accomplishment—and I find myself having amazing difficulty determining what to say. The problem, however, lies not in being unable to identify any virtues in my parents' child-rearing practices, but in the inability to narrow them down to a mere few pages.

Being, admittedly, the most rebellious and "challenging" of the Aharoni children, I have a feeling I harbor a few extra stories of parental techniques used in our household. While I never went so far as to explicitly break the rules, I was the tester—the one who bent the rules to see how far they would go. I tested the waters to make a point. I walked out to the edge of the cliff for the thrill of it, but I never completely jumped off. But instead of becoming a complete anarchist and rejecter of authority, my feisty tendencies were honed into a passion for philosophy and justice, and a quest to question everything and change the world for the better. How did this happen? What subtle parenting turned this spark into a passion instead of a forest fire?

My mother, in the wise words that precede my own, has already mentioned many factors that I find incredibly important as to what made me who I am. These concepts are often overlooked by many—if not most—other parents I've witnessed in my lifetime. Many of the ideas in this book, in one sense or other, have to do with the profound sense of trust and freedom our parents privileged us with.

When my friends were staying out until 3 A.M to rebel

against their parents' arbitrary 10 P.M. curfew, I was home by midnight so my parents wouldn't worry about me. As my friends repeatedly made the same mistakes and repeatedly got grounded for them (no matter what the offense), I was brainstorming with my mother what new, educational, appropriate, and relevant punishment I would fulfill. When my friends were cursing their parents' names for a verdict they felt was unfair, I was doing all in my power to earn—and keep—my parents' trust.

My parents treated me as an adult who was perfectly prepared—intellectually and morally—to make the right decisions. If I did not, I wouldn't care how many dishes I had to wash or papers I had to write or formal apologies I had to give. All I wanted was my parents' trust back—trust that I was still a good person. Trust that I was living the best life I could be living, as the best person I possibly could be. Imagining that my parents could think less of me as a person was the worst punishment I ever could have conjured.

My parents always encouraged my siblings and me to be our true selves—and to be proud to be different. Growing up in a pink house and driving a series of banana-yellow cars were a great foundation for our funky-socked, red-lipstick, ties-for-belts high school days. My parents encouraged us to be involved, but never forced us (resulting in me being the only kid I've ever heard of who had to *beg* for piano lessons). They never said "Why didn't you get an 'A'?" But only "Did you do your best?" They never said "No—because I said so!" But only "I'd really prefer you didn't do that because...."

Our house was never a house of strict rules with two bosses who were always right and three children who were supposed to obey their every whim on faith alone. Ours was a house of compromise, discussion, and challenge—where the parents were as open to lessons and growth as the kids were expected to be. There is no doubt in my mind that my interest in the field of law is due entirely to my ability and freedom to question and challenge everything. I grew up knowing that if I disagreed with my parents, I would be given the opportunity to present my case clearly and logically. As I grew older, more compromises were made. Even if I did not get my way, I was satisfied with the knowledge that my parents cared enough to listen to my opinion and consider it regarding every decision. They let me be my own third parent.

While I have been blessed with two incredible brothers to emulate, live up to, and help be raised by, my mother has missed discussing what I feel is the most important thing my parents have given their children: the gift of being role models themselves. Everywhere around me, I see messed-up parents trying to raise good kids and wondering what's going wrong. Communication-challenged parents wondering why they cannot hold a decent conversation with their children. Mothers who allow their husbands to treat them badly wondering why their sons don't respect women or their daughters only date macho jerks. Dysfunctional marriages whose partners wonder why their children go through significant others like coffee filters, or sleep around too often to have time for a healthy relationship with a steady boyfriend or girlfriend.

I have lost count of the people in my life—young and old, acquaintances and long-time friends—who have pulled me aside to tell me how much they adored and admired my parents. My parents didn't just tell us to give our spare change to the homeless, they gave their money and time to charities and people in need. They didn't just tell us to give everyone a chance, but they befriended and introduced us to every type of person you can imagine. They were the first ones to strike up a conversation with the one person in the room who looked like he just didn't belong.

My parents showed us time and time again, by buying us ice cream to celebrate a good day or taking us on a vacation to show us the world, that quality of life and doing the right thing are more important than money or possessions. They demonstrated to us that life experience and helping others are more important than a fat wallet or a prestigious title. They illustrated, through 37 years of marriage, what a healthy relationship should look like, and how we should treat (and deserve to be treated by) our spouses. They are humble, kind, loving, and strong.

My parents inadvertently have given my brothers and me the most precious thing they ever could have—proof that there are truly good people in the world. They are living images of the people we would like to become. To raise a good person, you must be a good person. And never a day goes by that I do not feel blessed to be a part of our family and honored to be able to call such amazing people "Mom" and "Dad."

—GALIA AHARONI

"THE ONLY RATIONAL WAY OF
EDUCATING A CHILD IS TO BE AN
EXAMPLE—OF WHAT TO AVOID,
IF ONE CAN'T BE THE OTHER
SORT."
—ALBERT EINSTEIN

ABOUT THE AUTHOR

Now that the last of her three children is out of the house and on her own, author Nesta Aharoni can honestly say that she has raised three good kids. She has never suffered a sleepless night worrying about her children. From the time they were little, they were trusted to do the right thing. And they have never disappointed her. *My Goodness: My Kids* is the author's response to all of the parents who continually ask her how she did it—no alcohol, no violence, no drugs, no sex. No hurting a friend. No disrespecting a parent. Common sense and intuition were the tools she used to raise three ethical, kind-hearted, contributing members of society.

A love of language has kept Nesta in the word business throughout her professional career. She began in the field of court reporting as a hearing reporter for many State Boards and Agencies. She then became a court reporting firm owner, an instructor of court reporting, and the director of a college court reporting program. She created an employment magazine with a partner, which won the Small Business of the Month award in San Diego. After the magazine was purchased by a larger publisher, Nesta remained on as its editor for nine years.

Nesta is a member of Publishers Marketing Association, Self Publishers Association of North America, and Publishers & Writers of San Diego. She has served on the state School Oversight Committee for the California Certified Shorthand Reporters Board, and on Mira Costa College's Business Department Virtual Business Advisory Board.

Nesta lives in Carlsbad, California, with her husband, Eitan. She is creating a series of Goodness titles. Please contact her to discover how you can participate in upcoming My Goodness projects.

YOUR NEXT STEP
JOIN THE NATIONAL GOODNESS MOVEMENT

Grassroots Publishing Group, Inc., is preparing a series of My Goodness books and is laying the groundwork for a **National Goodness Movement**. Here is how you can take your goodness plan a step further.

1. **Share** *My Goodness: My Kids* with a friend.
2. **Submit open-ended, scenario questions** that promote lively morality- and ethics-based discussion between adults and children. Your questions may be chosen for print in our upcoming **Companion Workbook**. The Companion Workbook will support a network of Play/Discussion Groups nationwide.
3. **Establish or join a My Goodness Play/Discussion Group** in your area. Discuss age-appropriate morality- and ethics-based situations with your group's kids and parents. Use the Companion Workbook as your guide.
4. **Contribute a story** that demonstrates how your child has learned a valuable lesson about goodness or demonstrated goodness in a meaningful way. Your story may be chosen for print in our upcoming **Your Goodness: Your Kids** follow-up book.
5. **Receive a Goodness Recognition Certificate** for your child by submitting a description of how he or she has demonstrated honorable behavior.
6. **Participate in our Good Kids Annual City Competition** by submitting, and encouraging others in your area to submit, stories of good kids displaying kindness, empathy, and integrity. Join us in celebrating the **Good Kids City of the Year**.
7. **Share My Goodness: My Kids Merchandise** with children, family, and friends.

Learn more at www.GrassrootsPublishingGroup.com